# EVERYDAY CHARACTERS

## An Alphabet Book of Fonts

Allie Fenelon

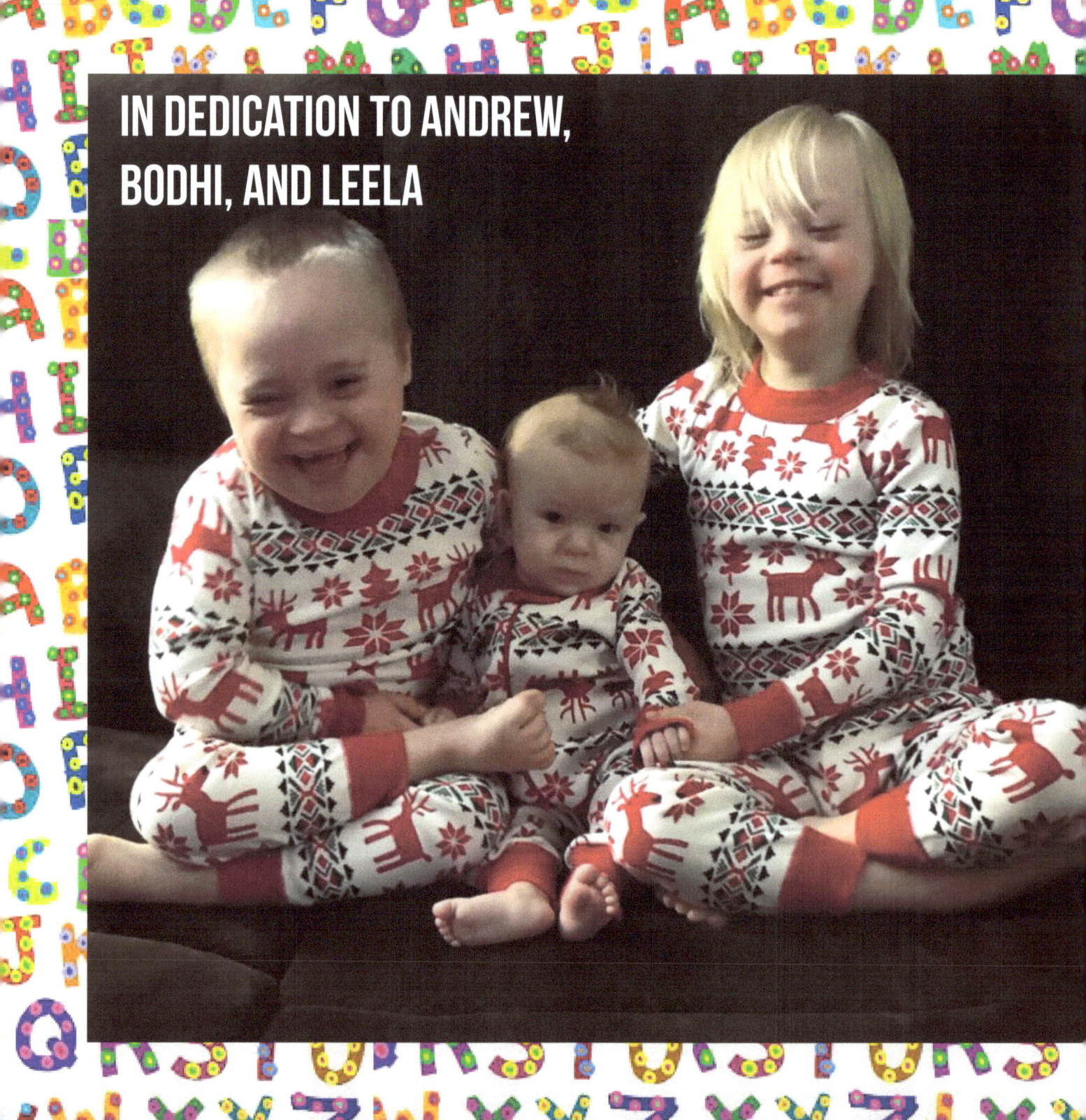

IN DEDICATION TO ANDREW, BODHI, AND LEELA

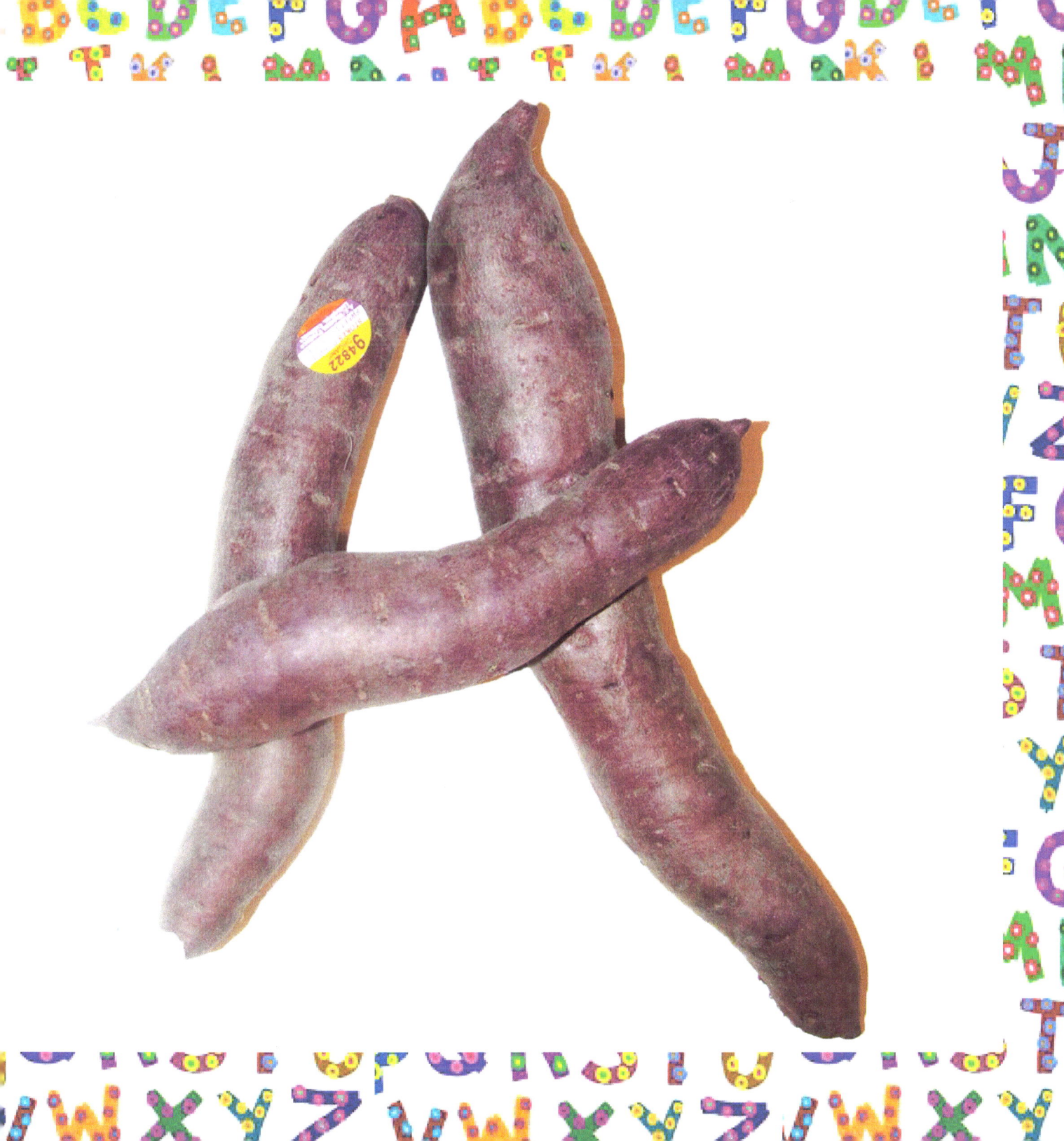

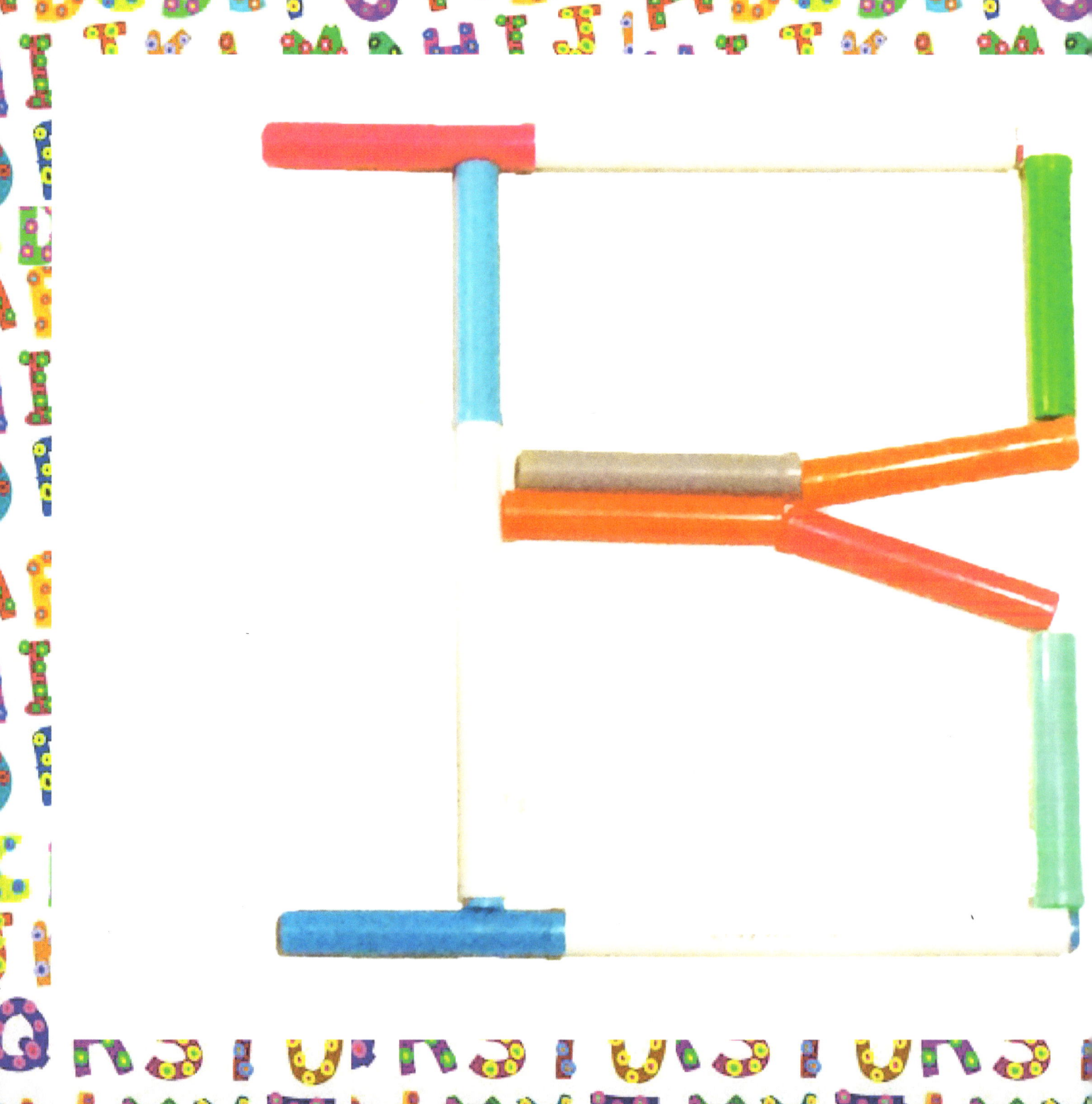

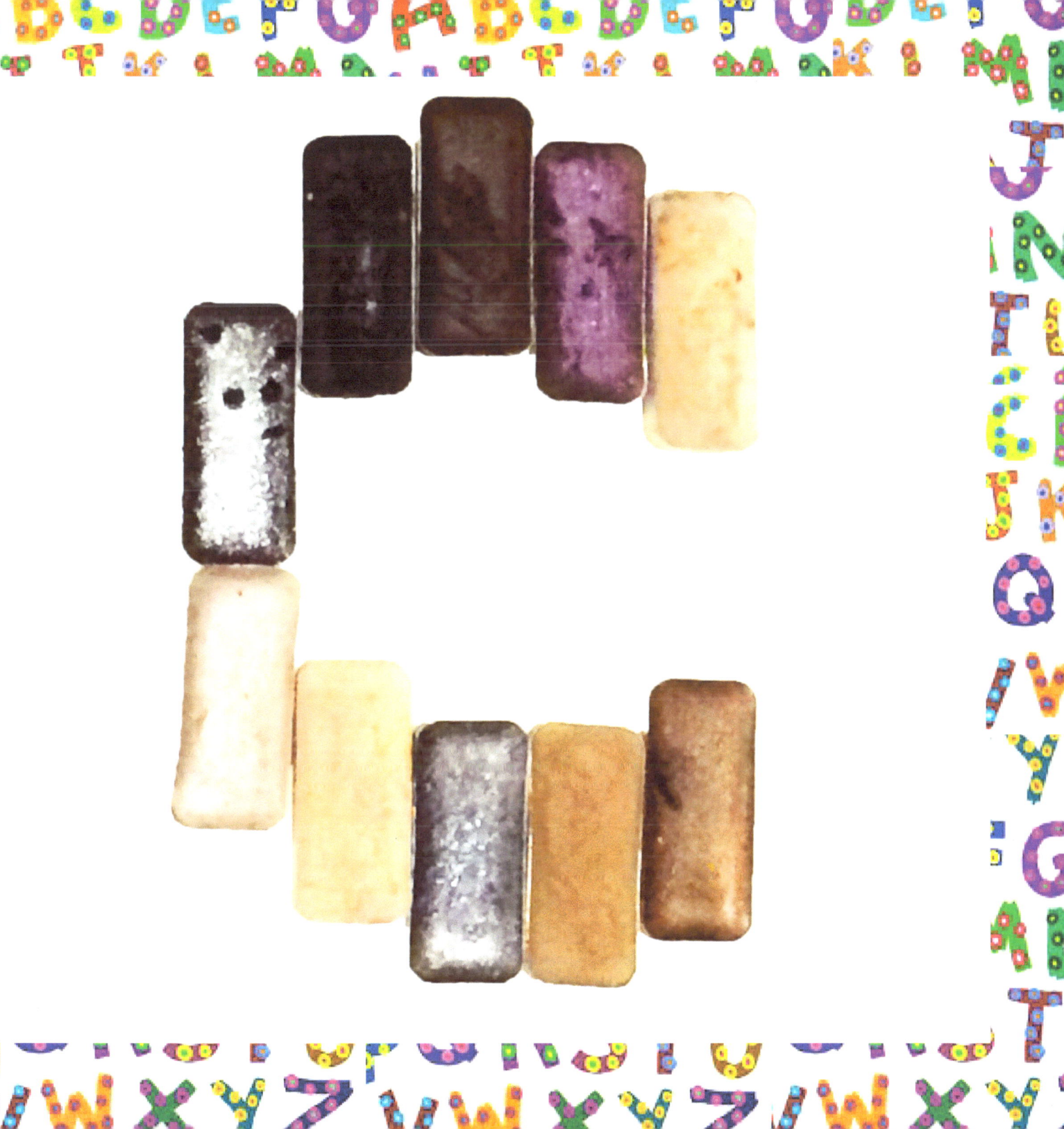

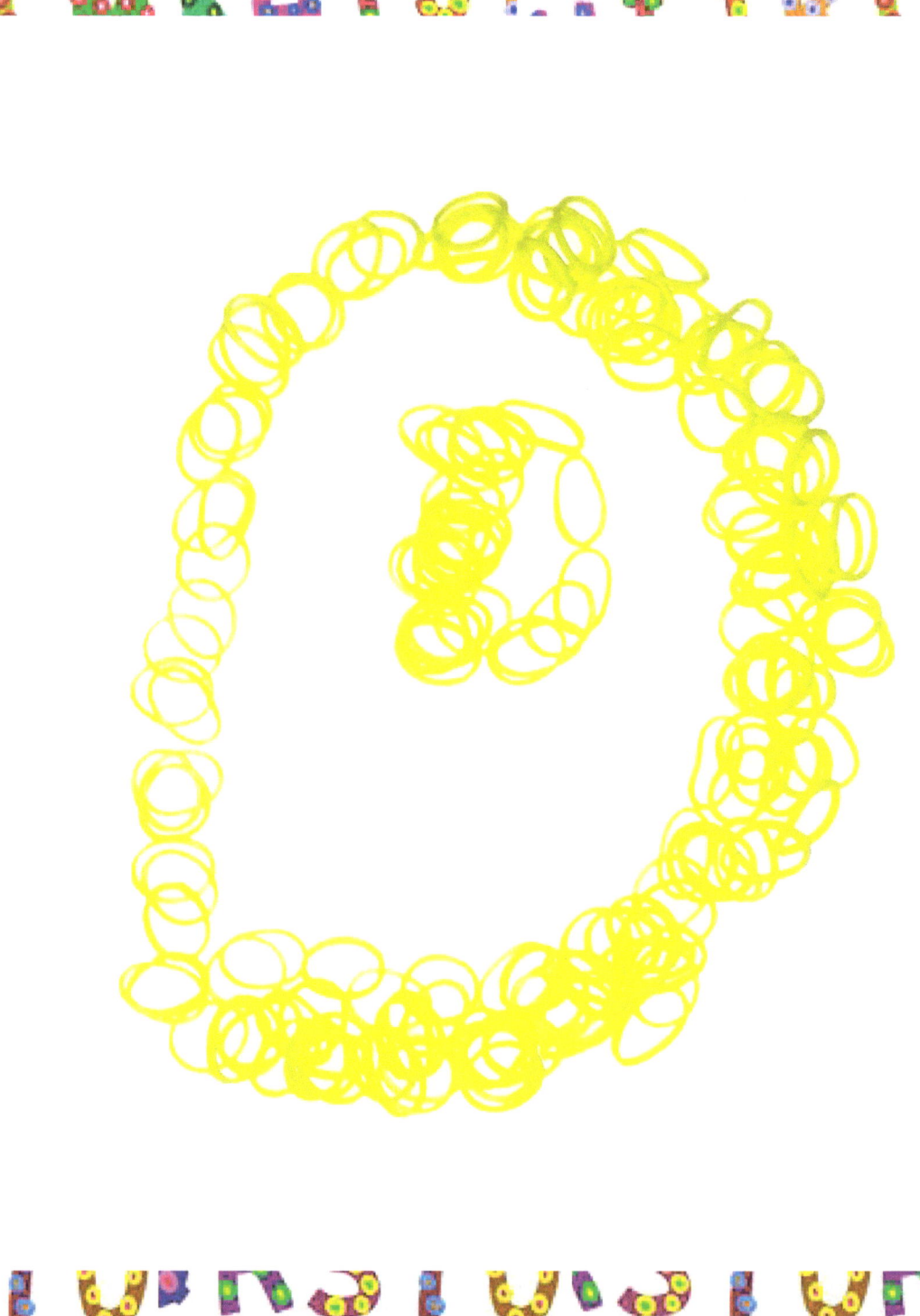

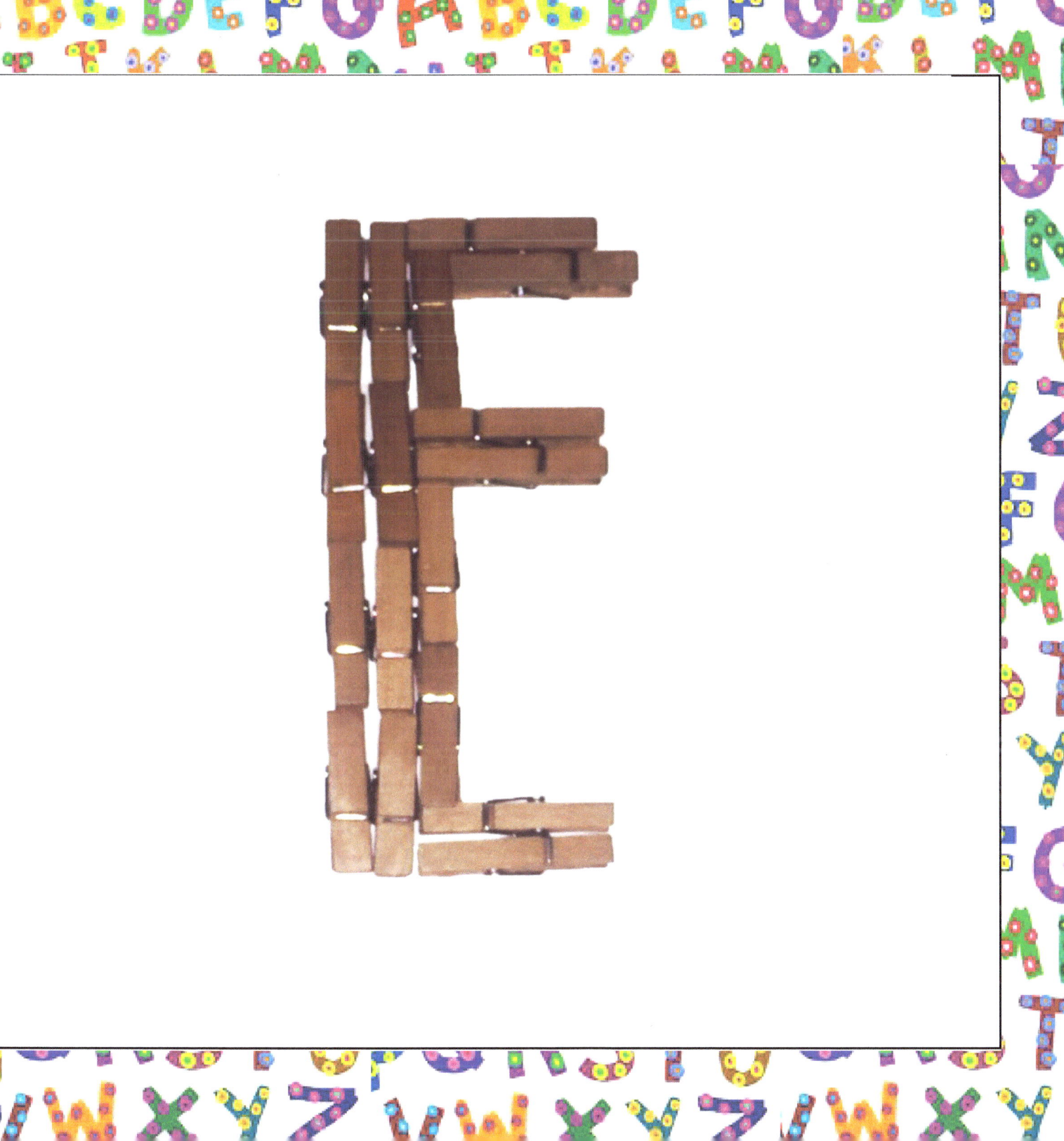

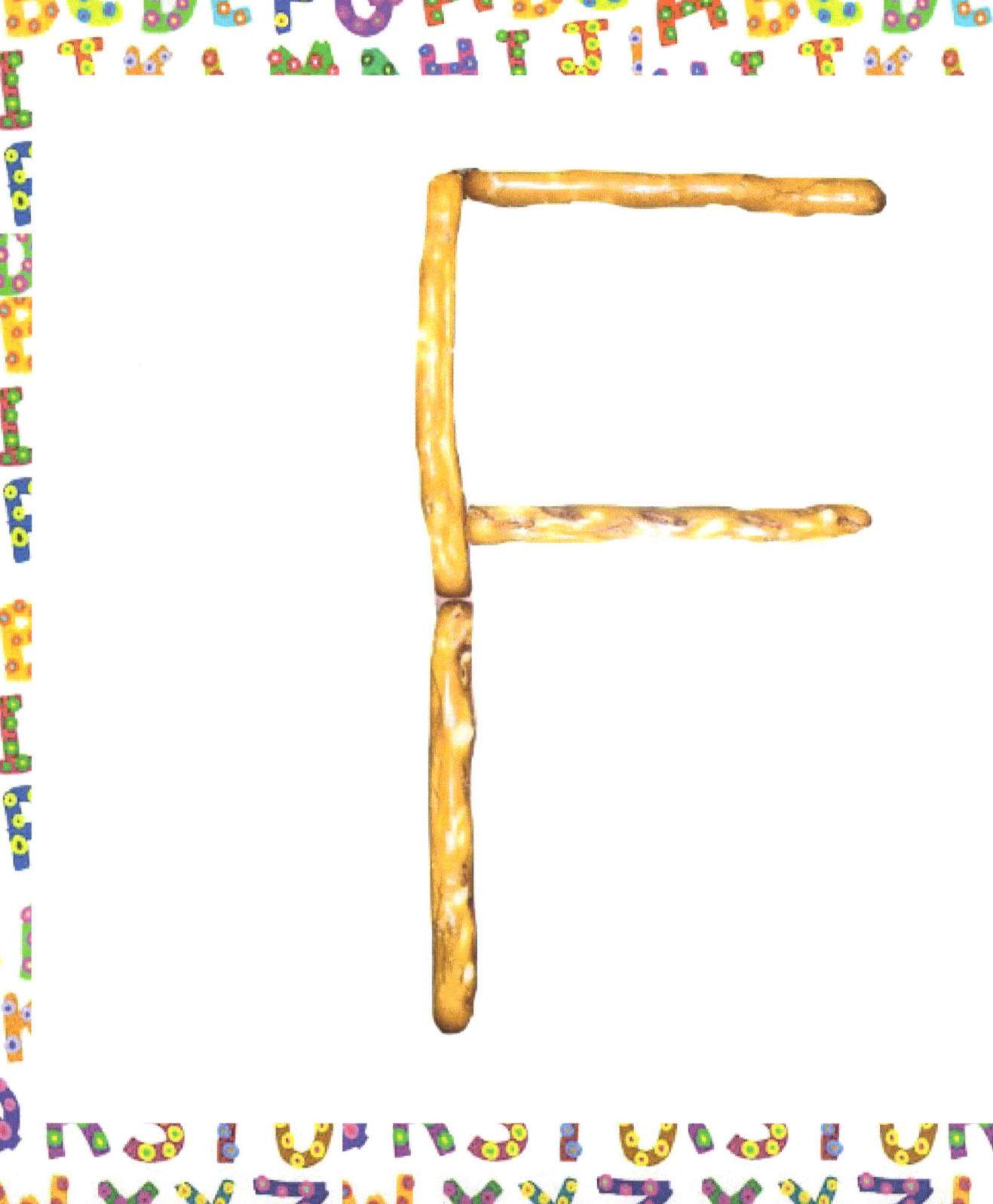

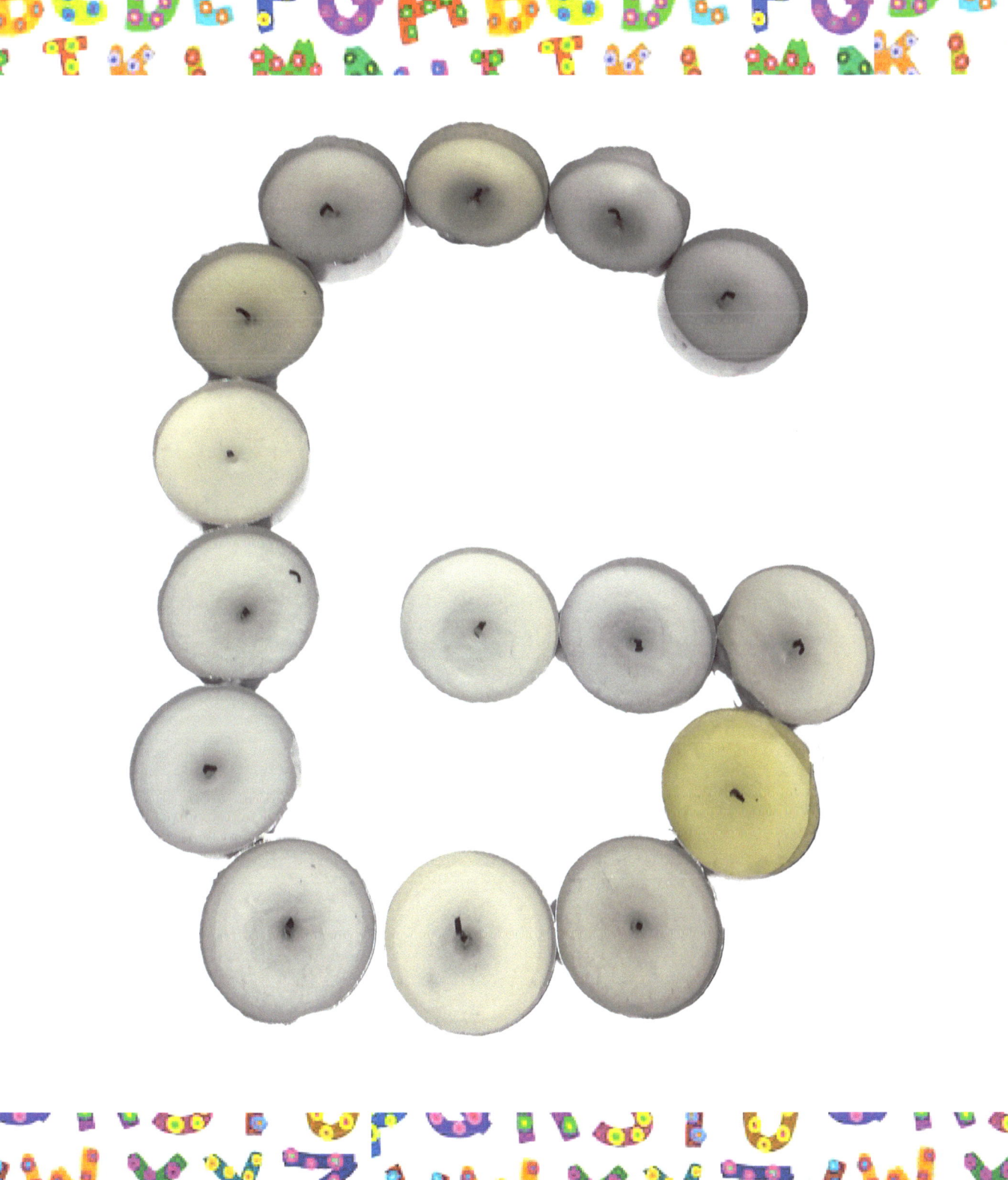

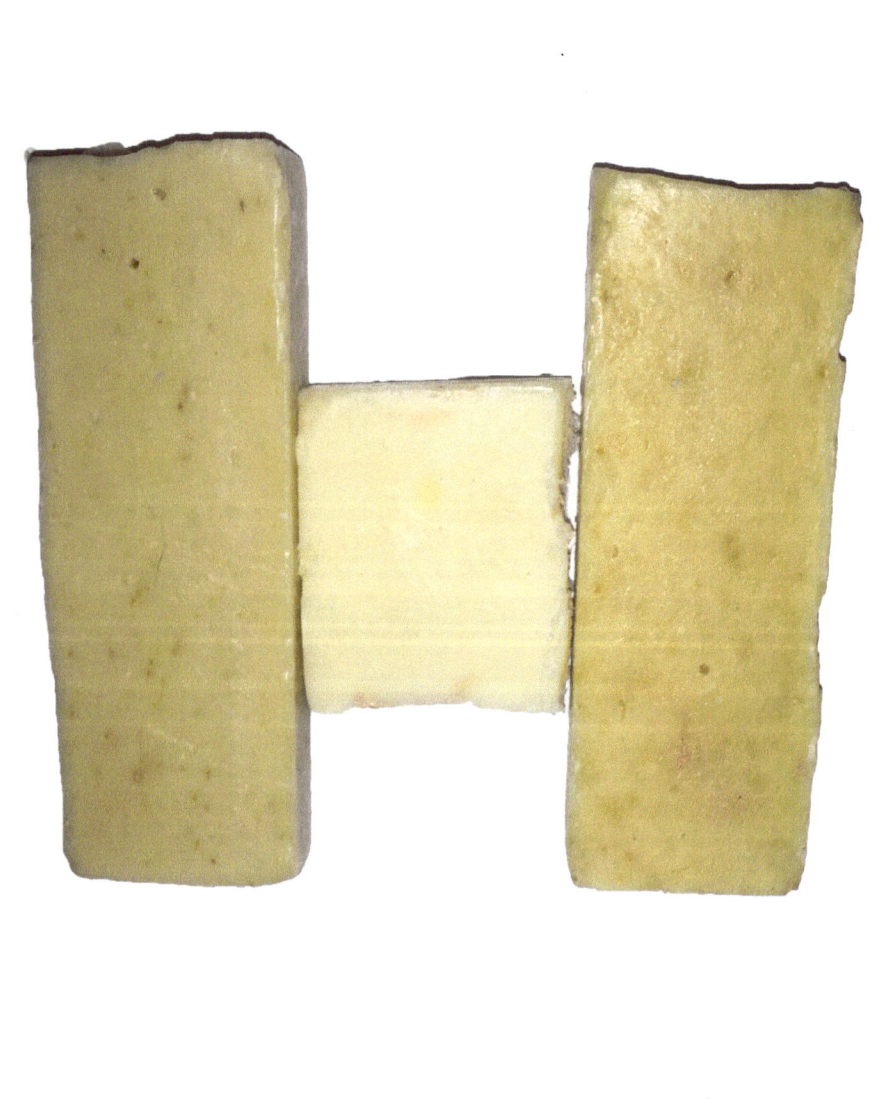

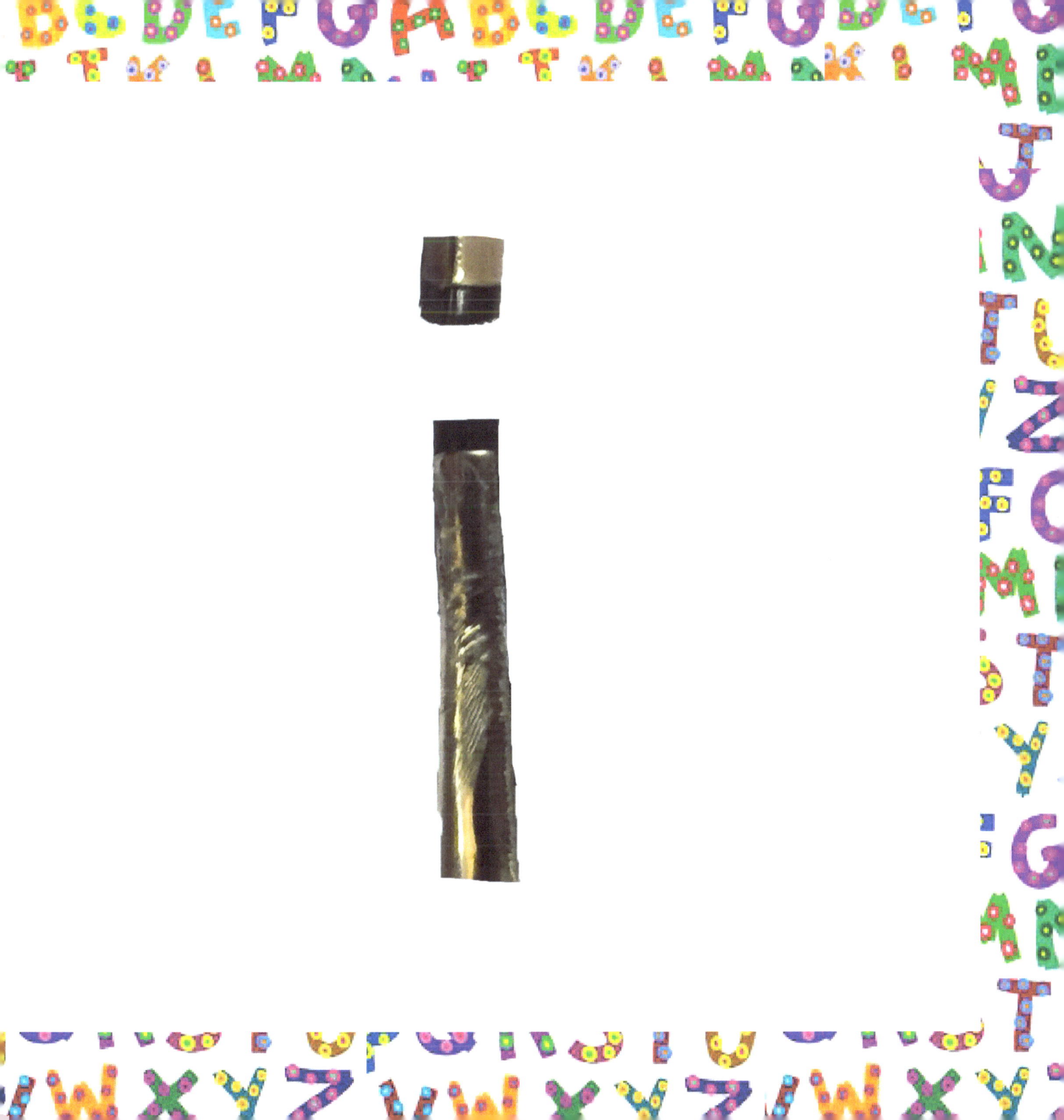

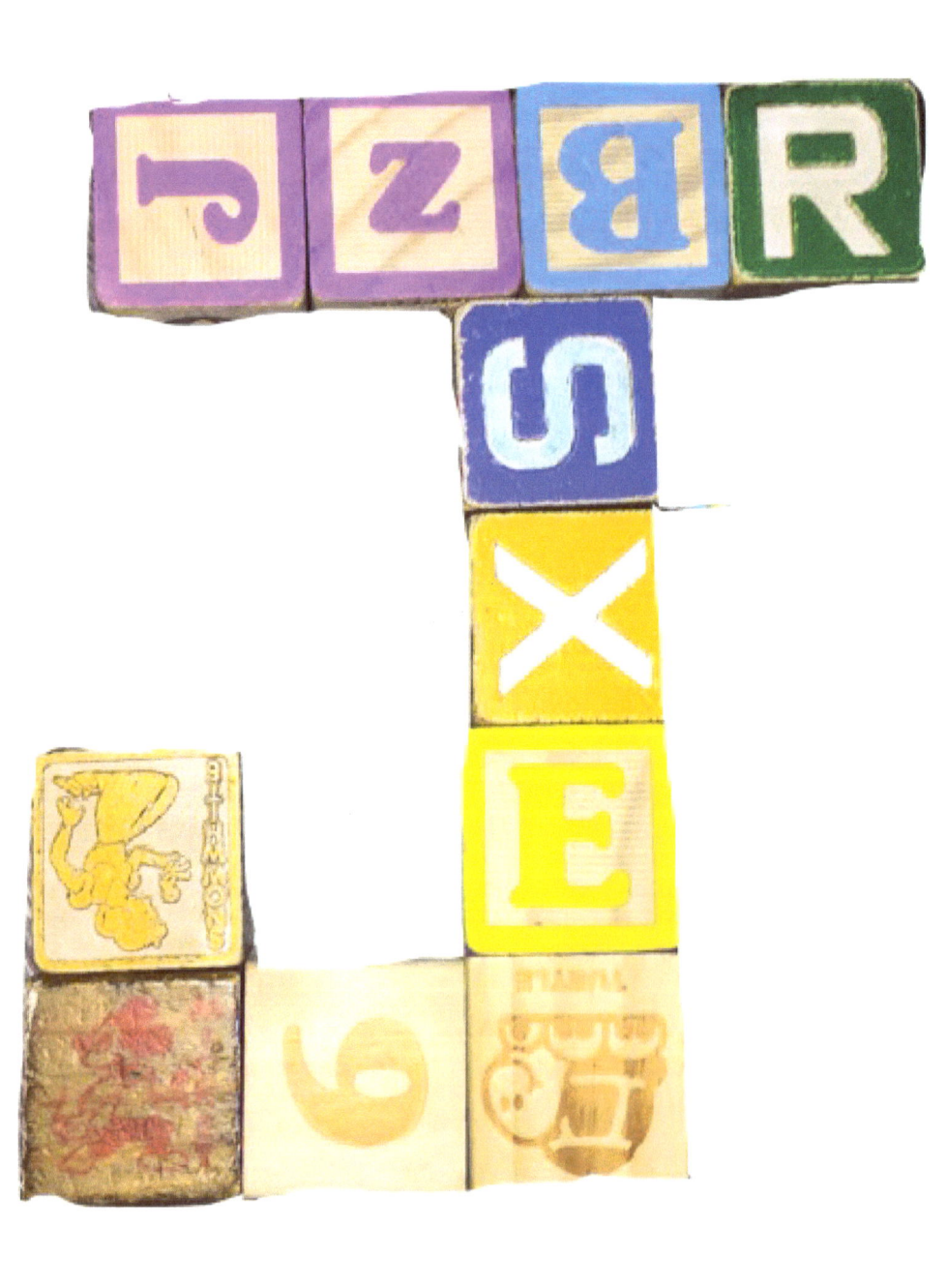

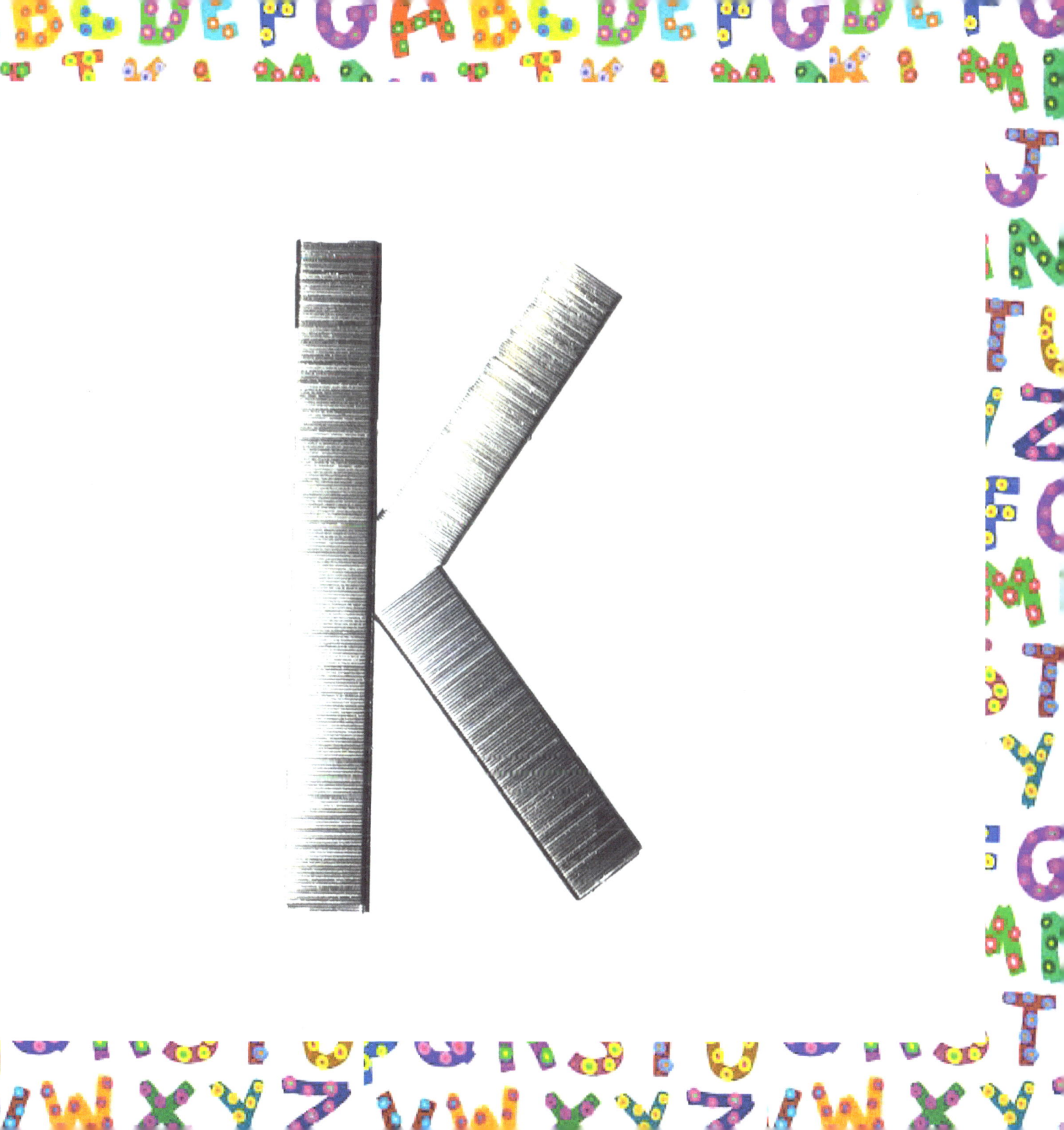

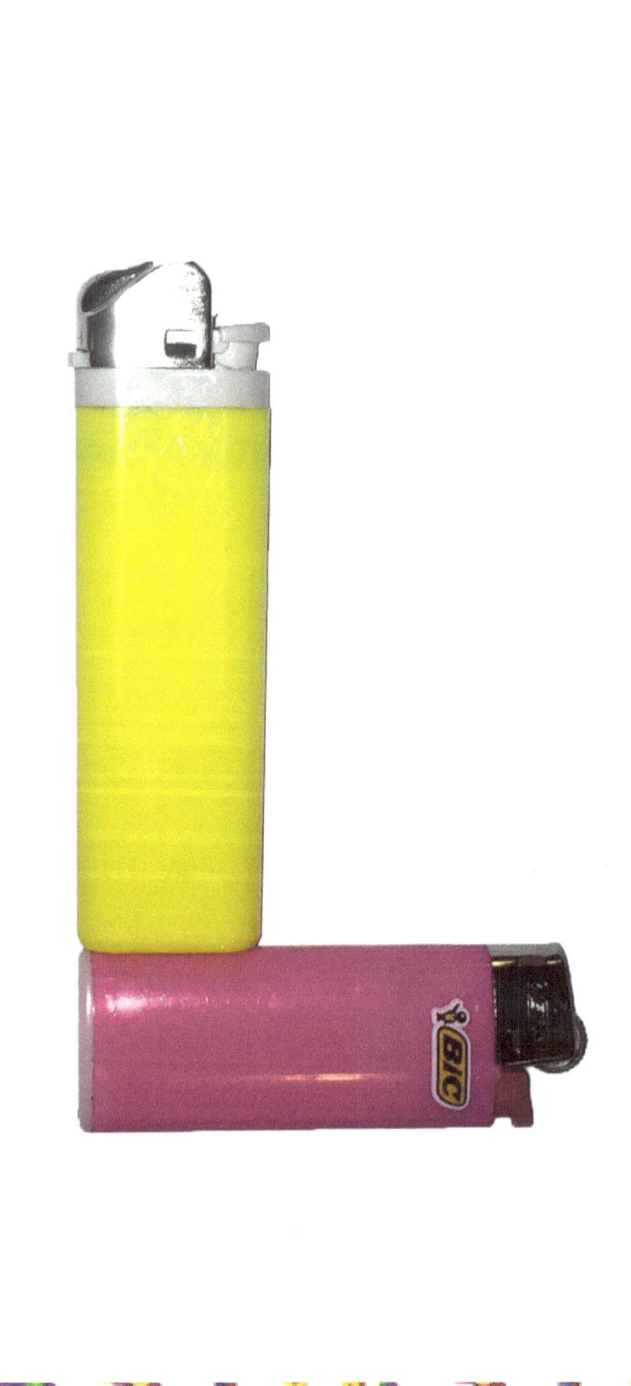

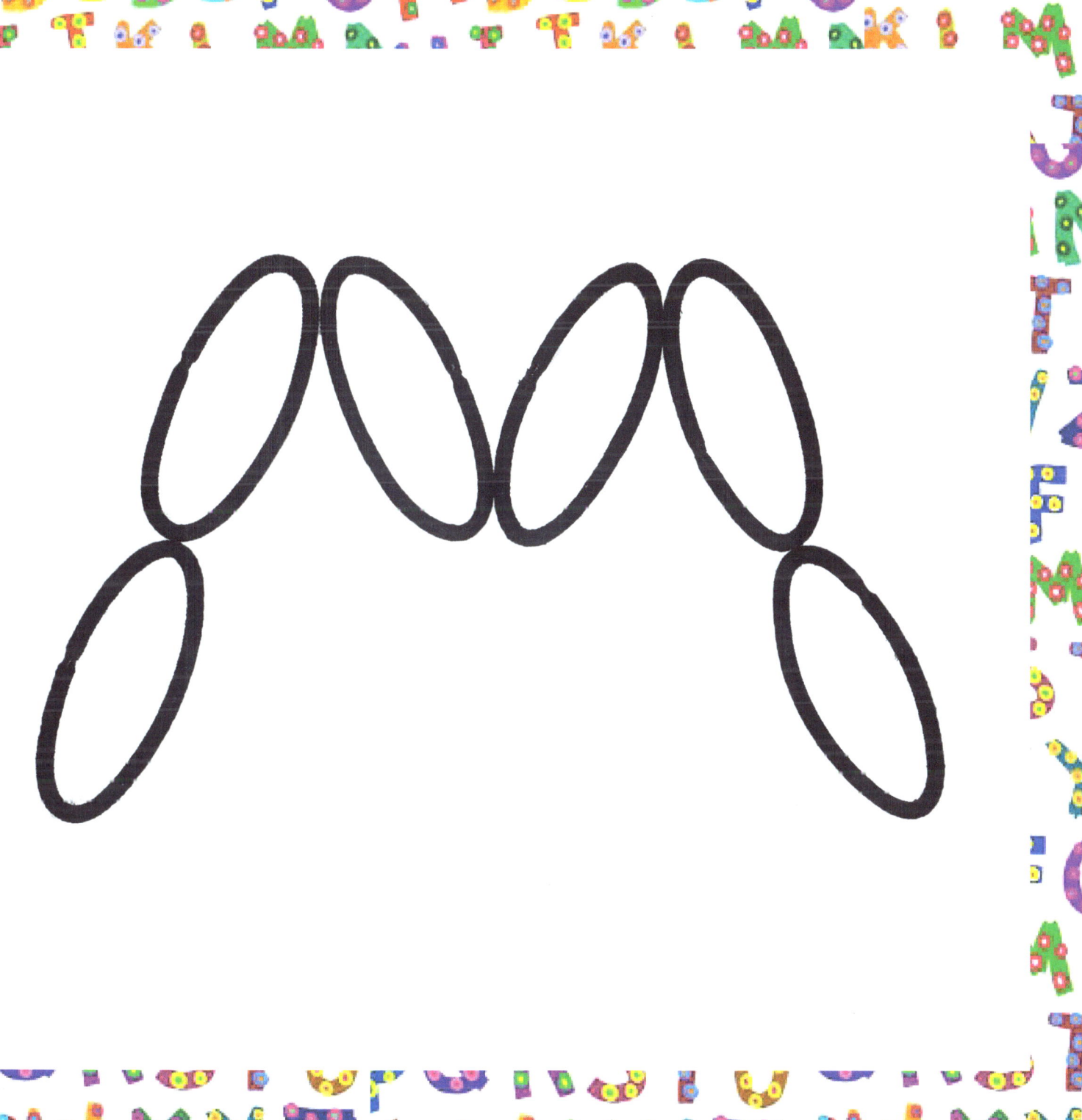

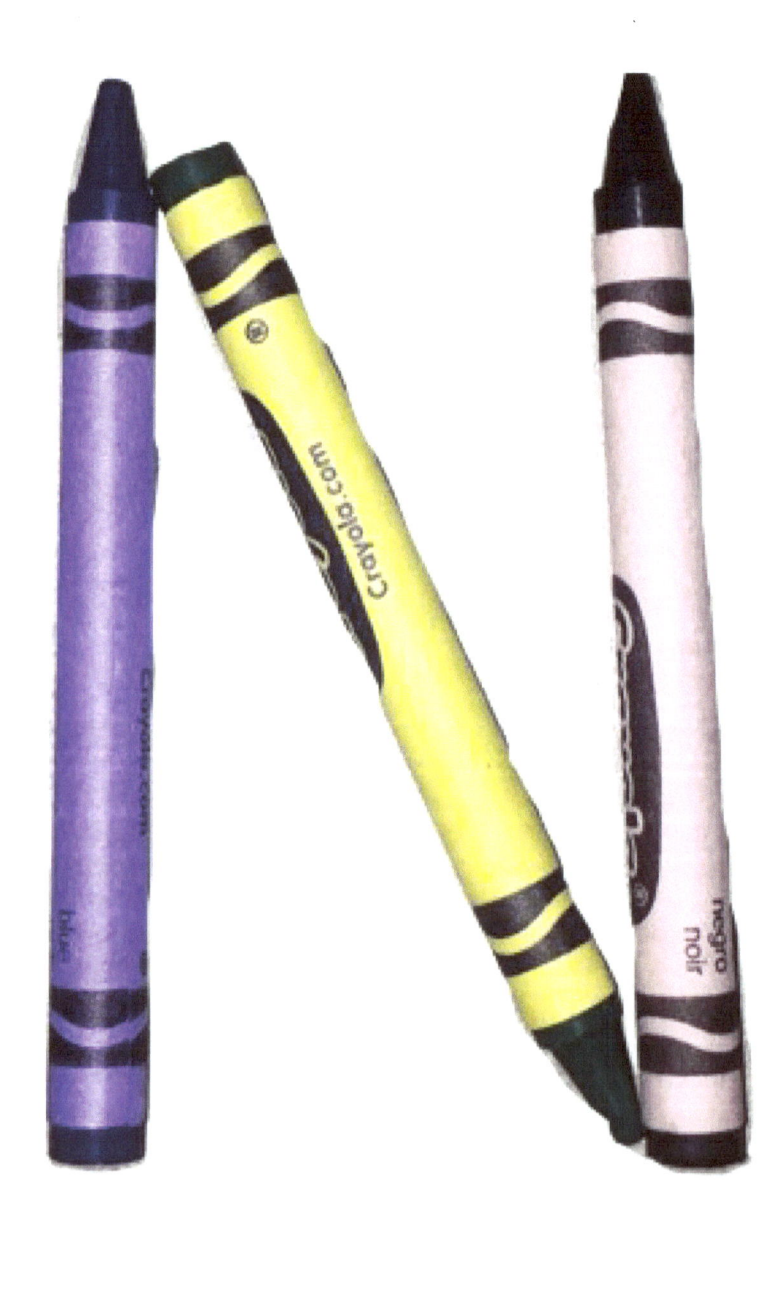

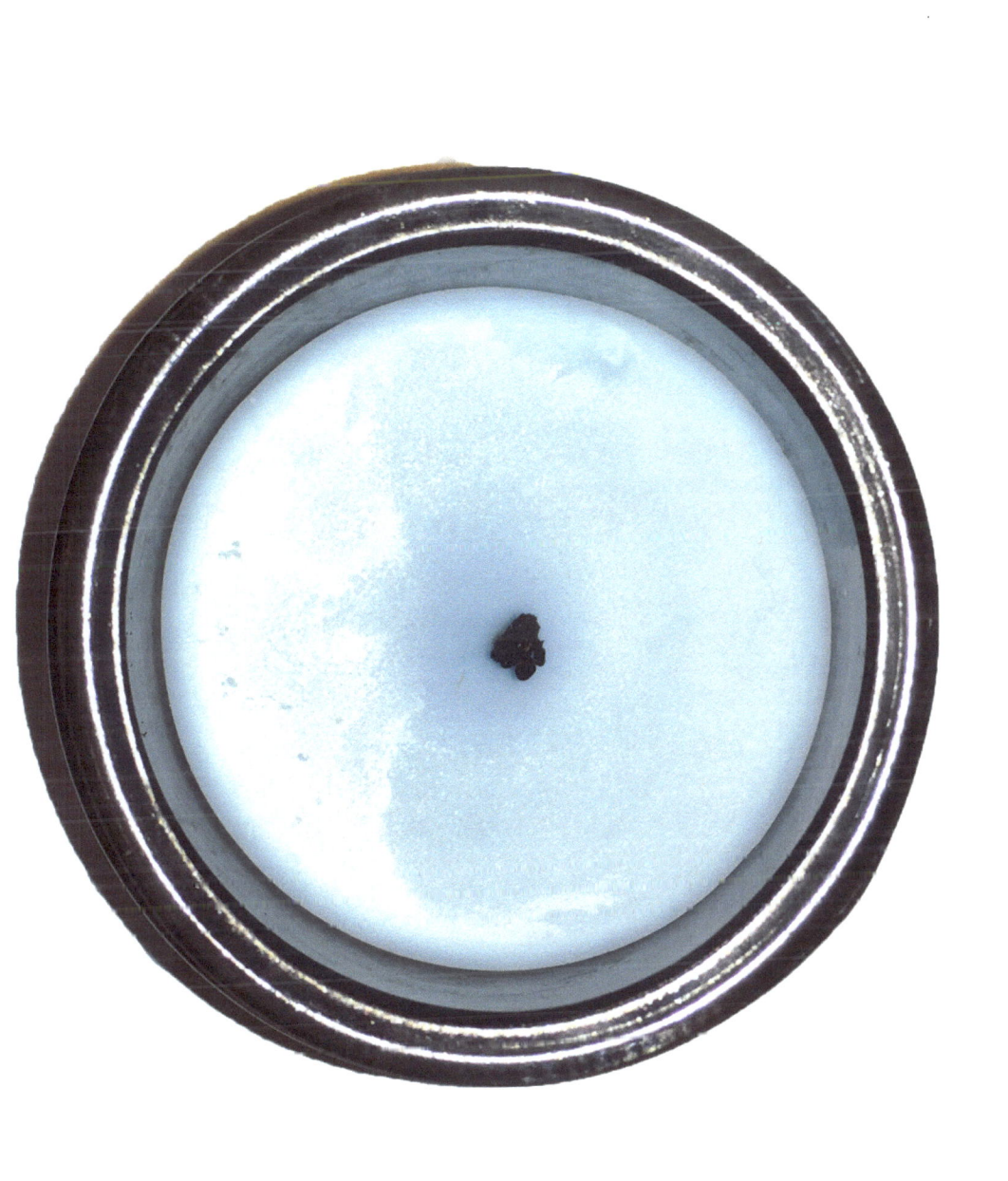

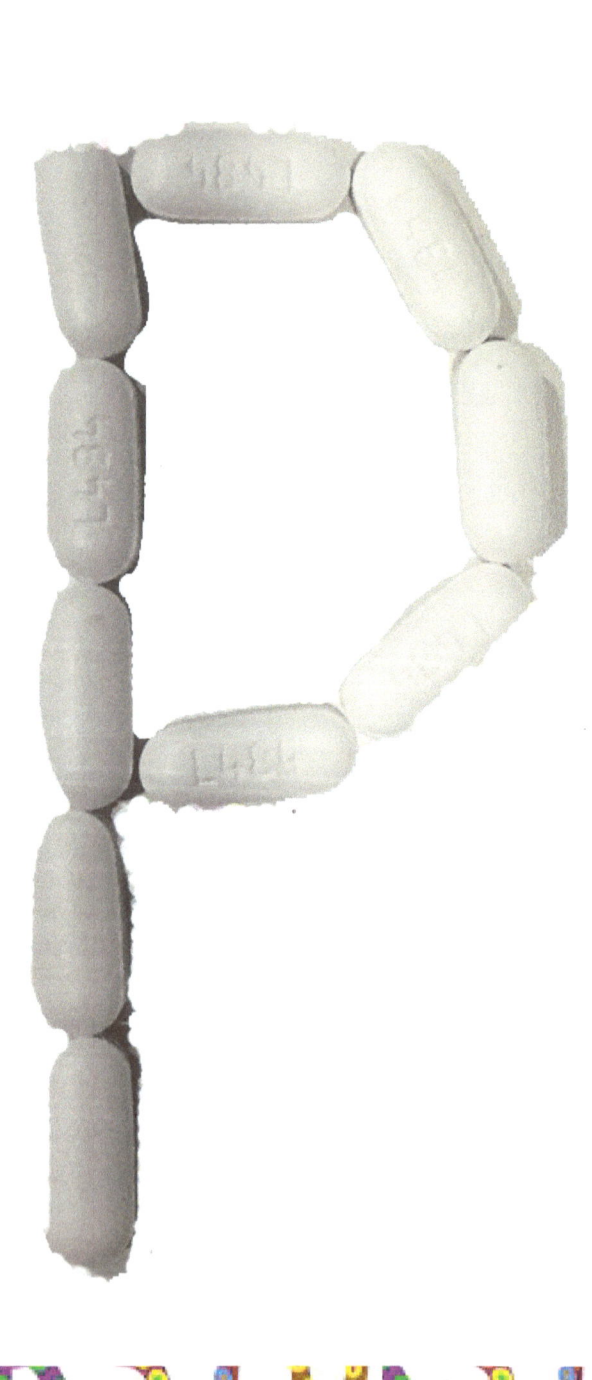

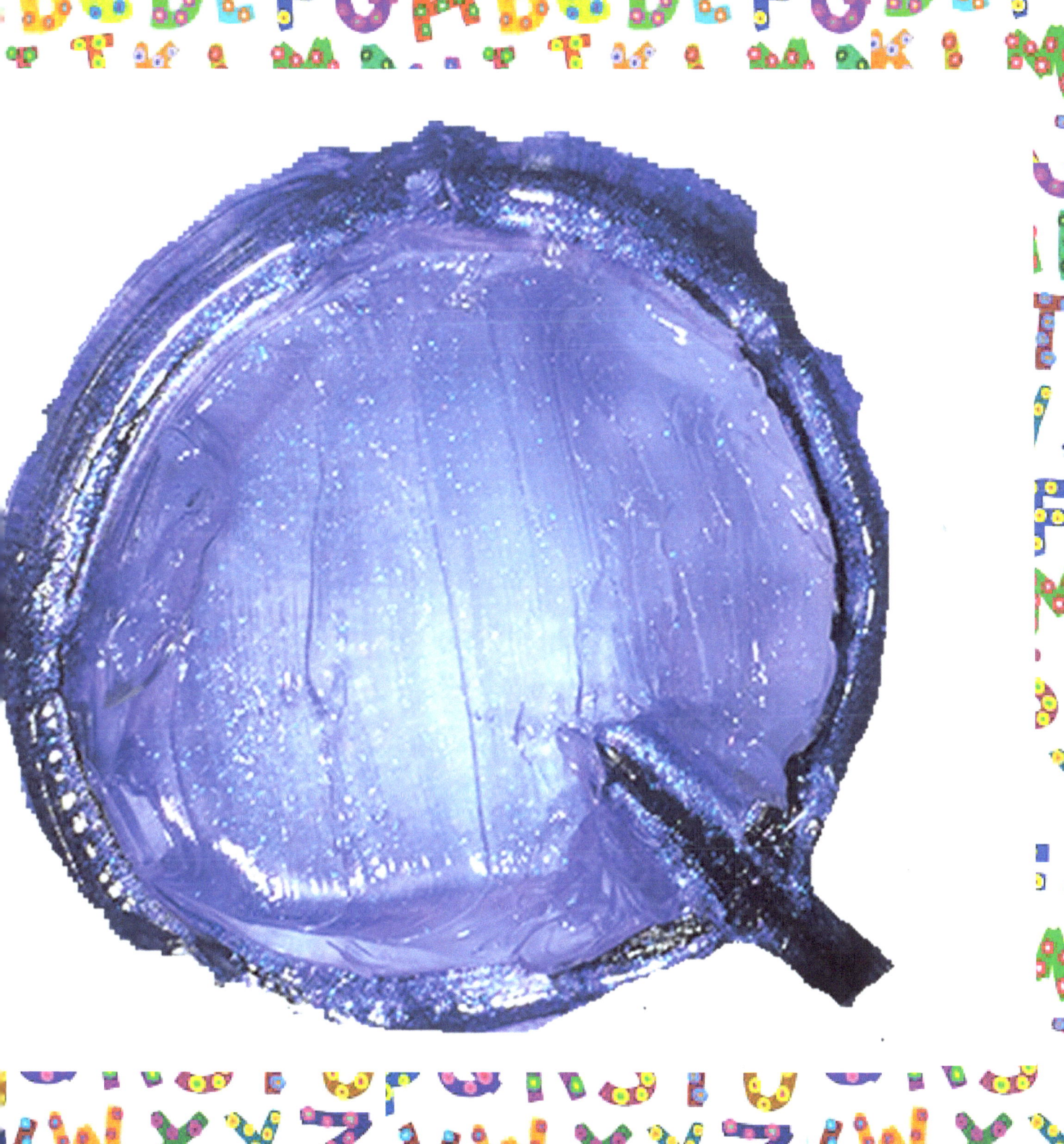

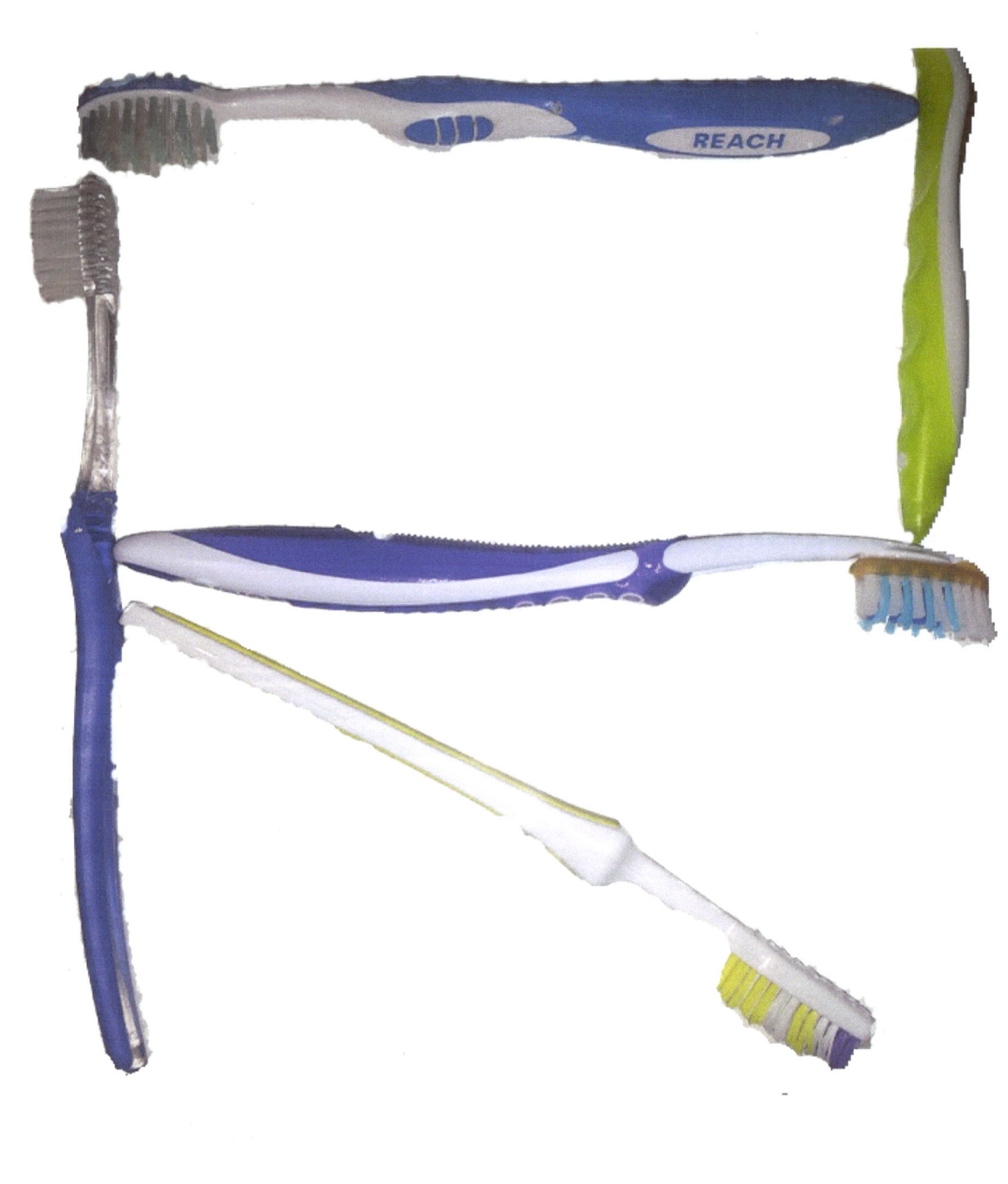

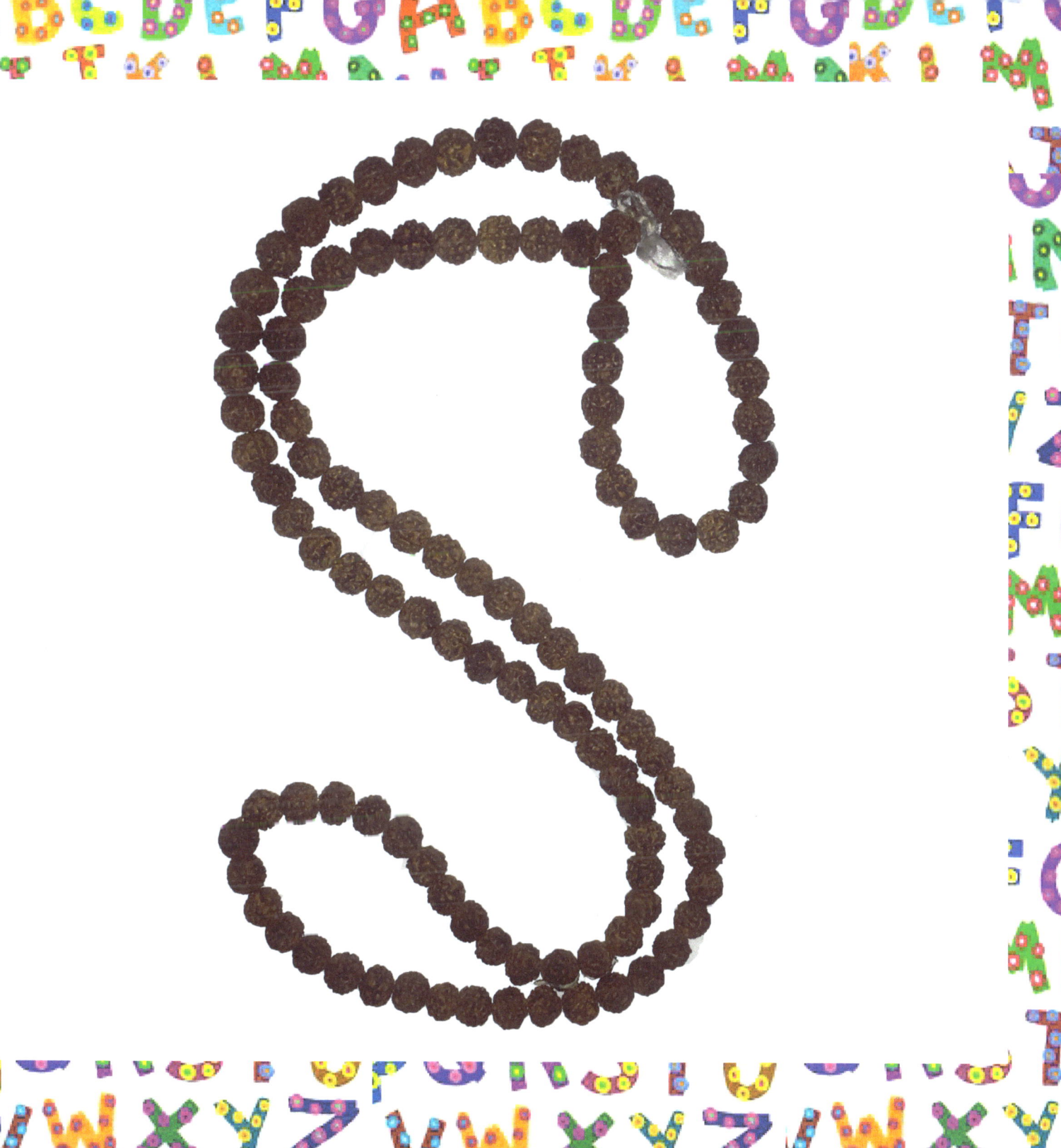

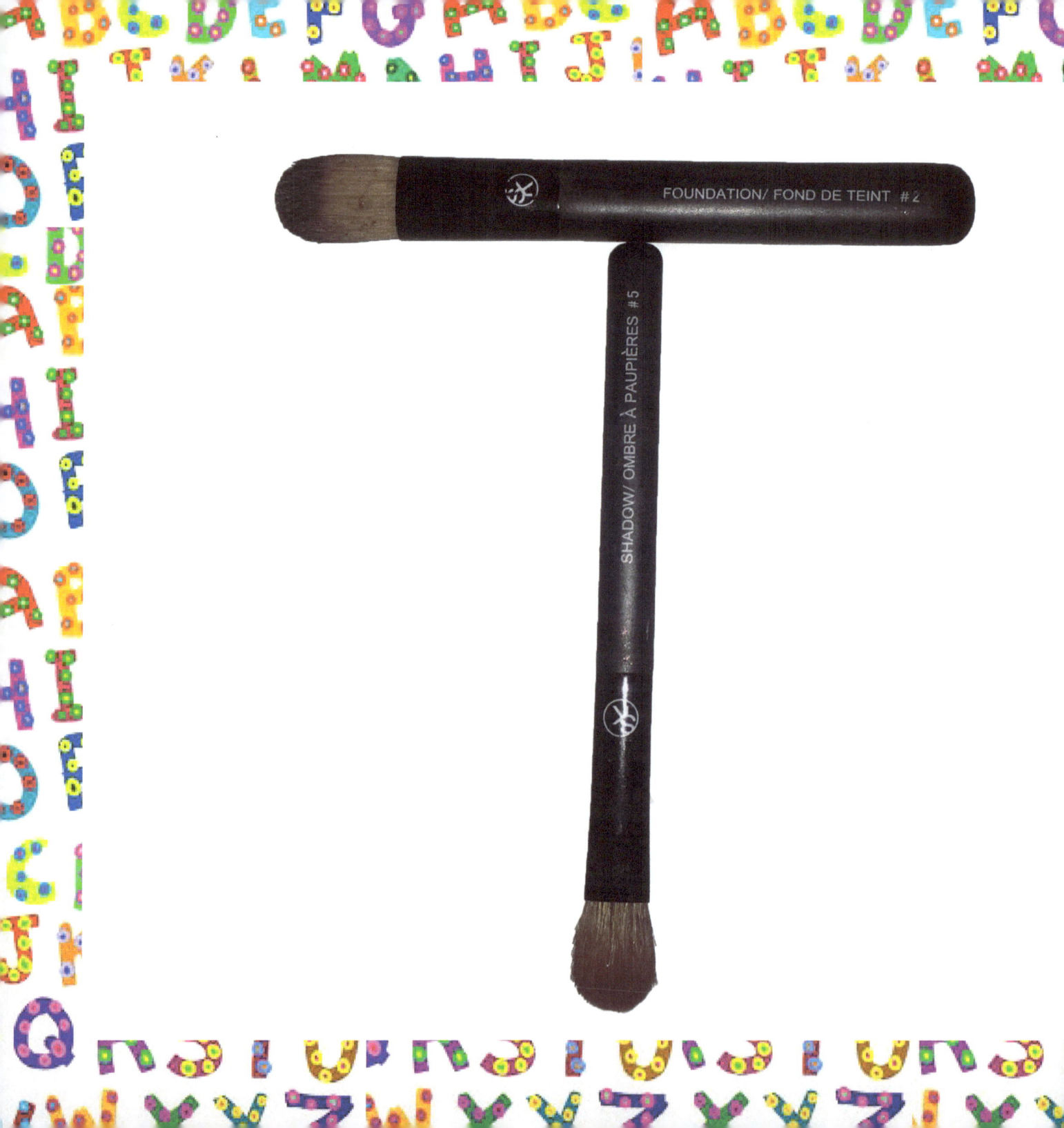

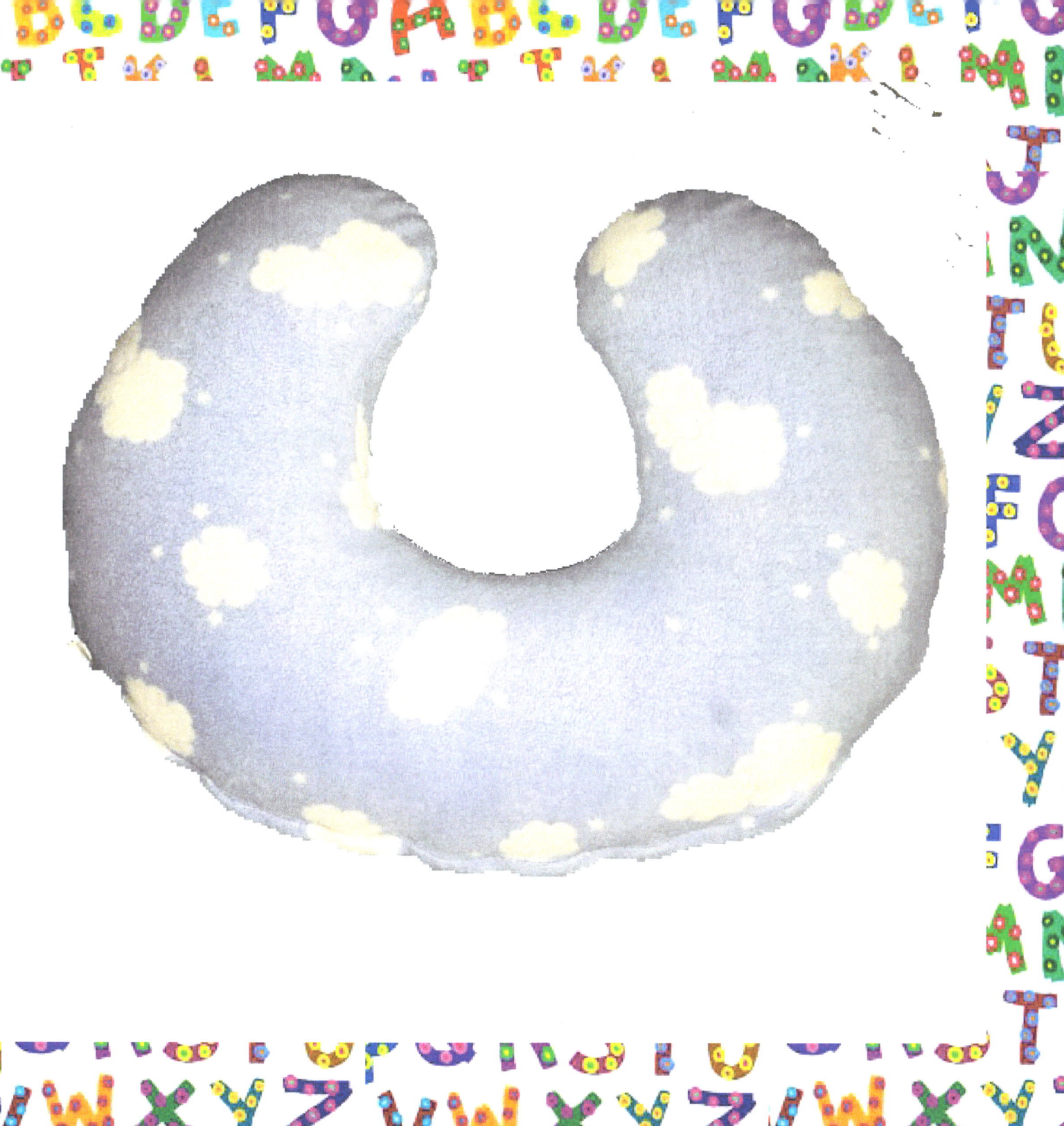

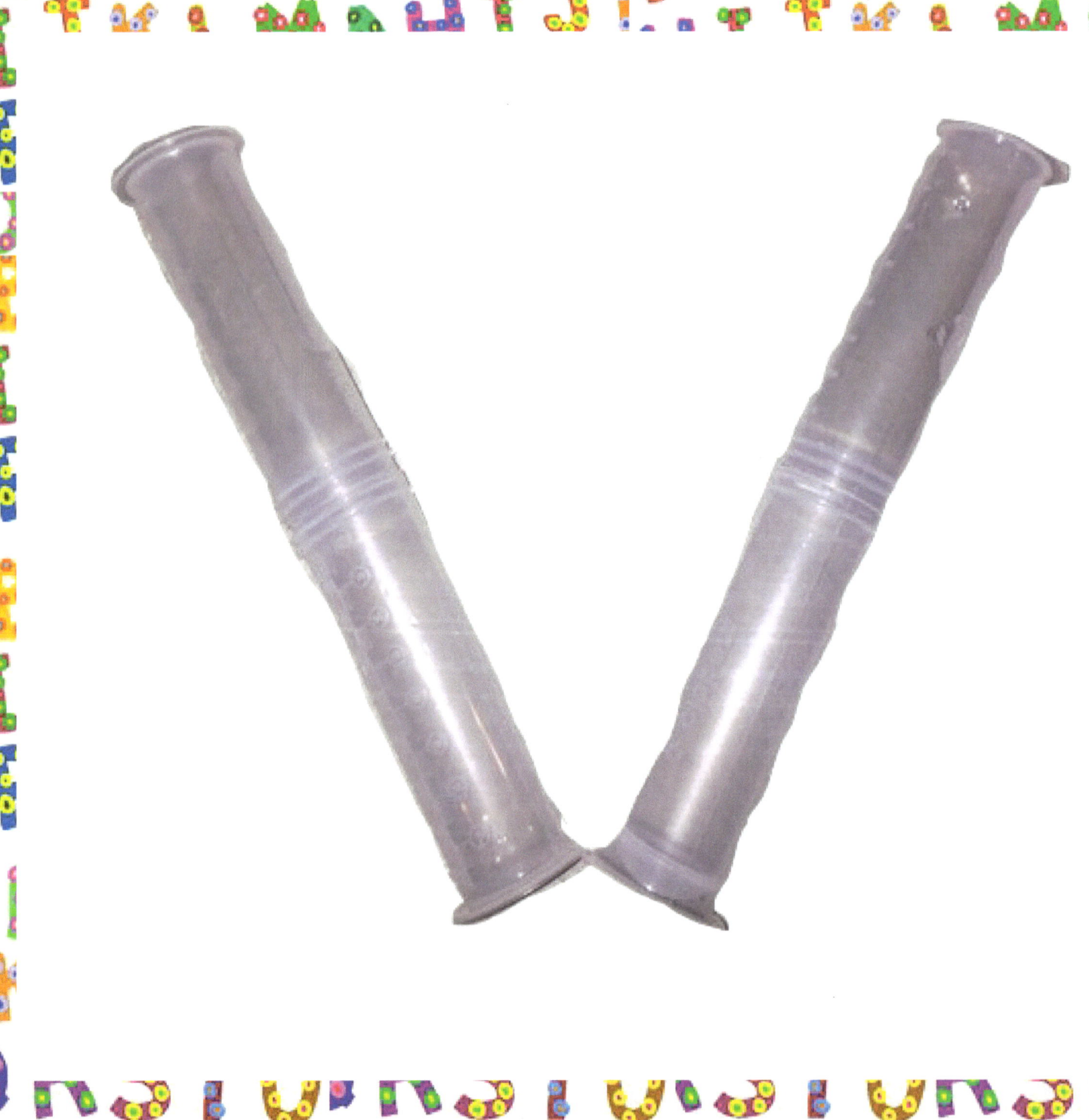

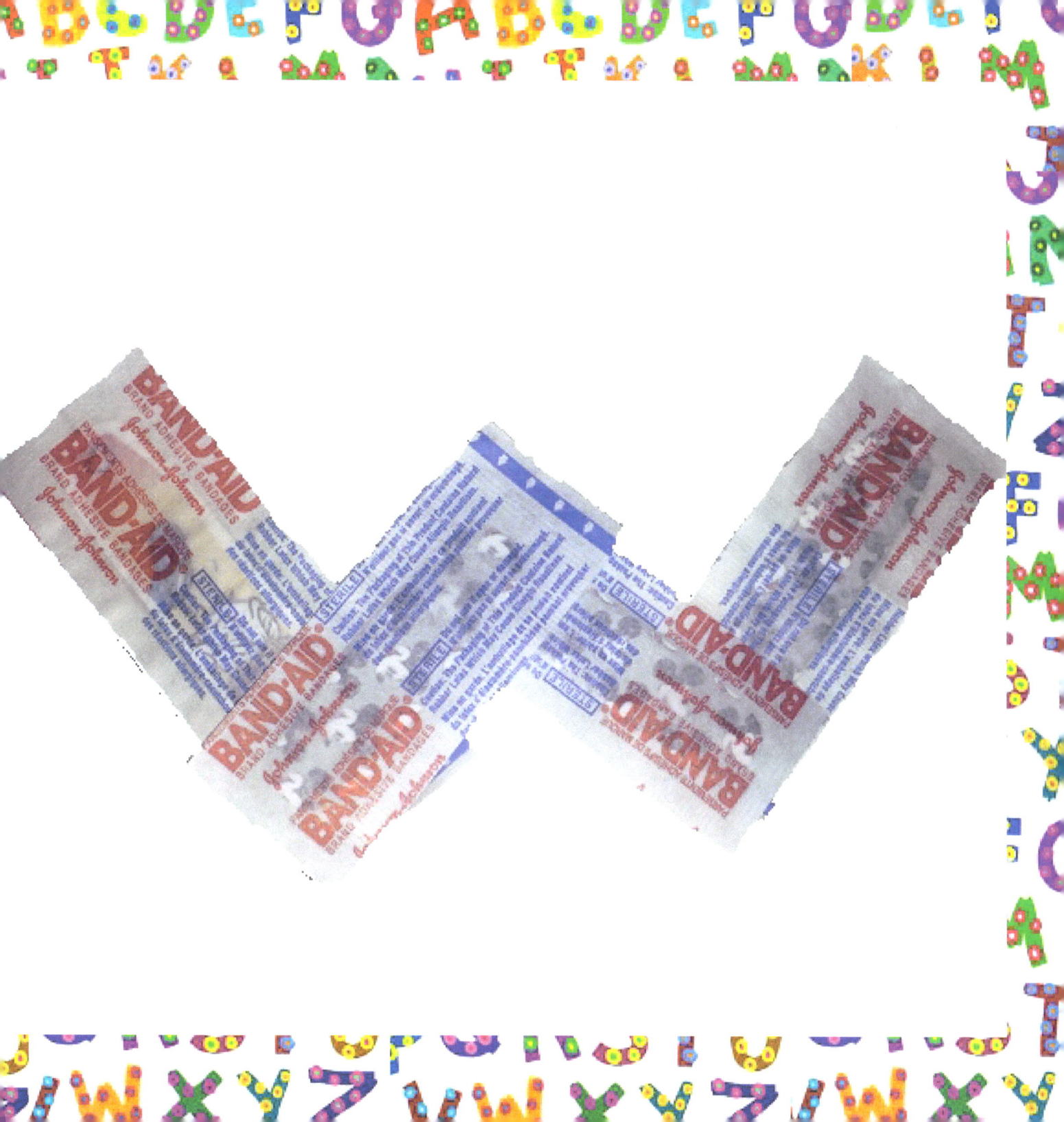

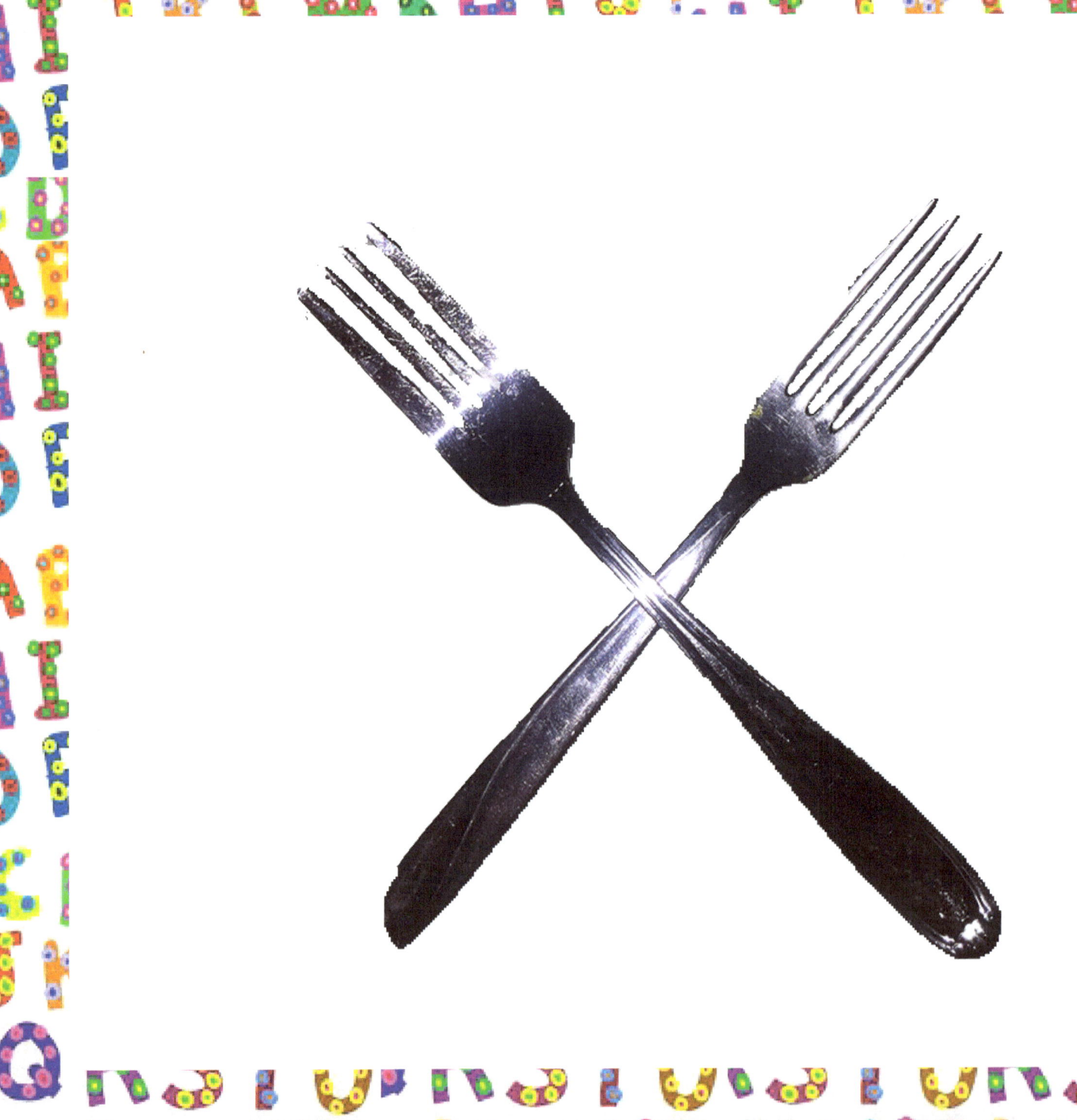

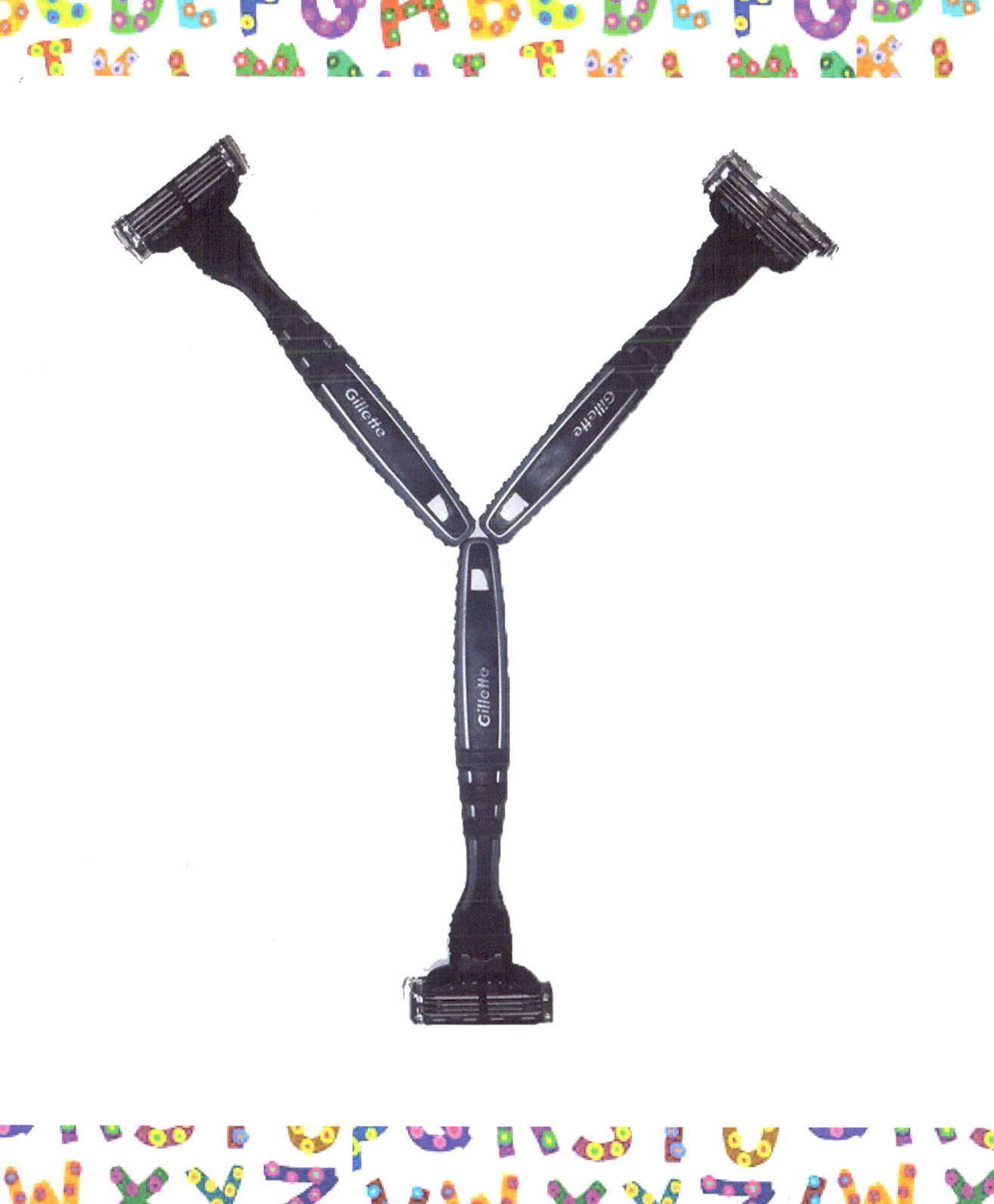

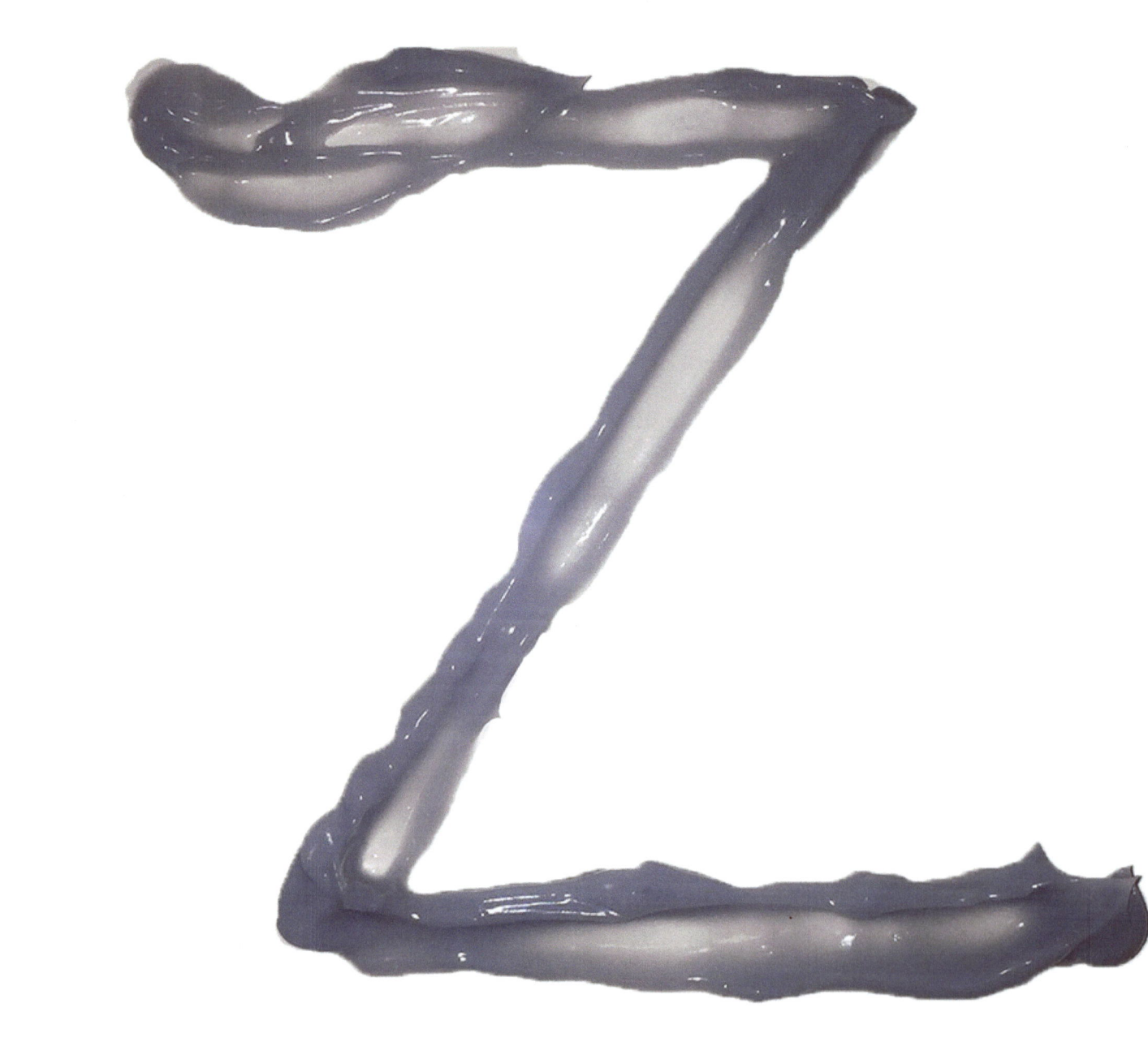

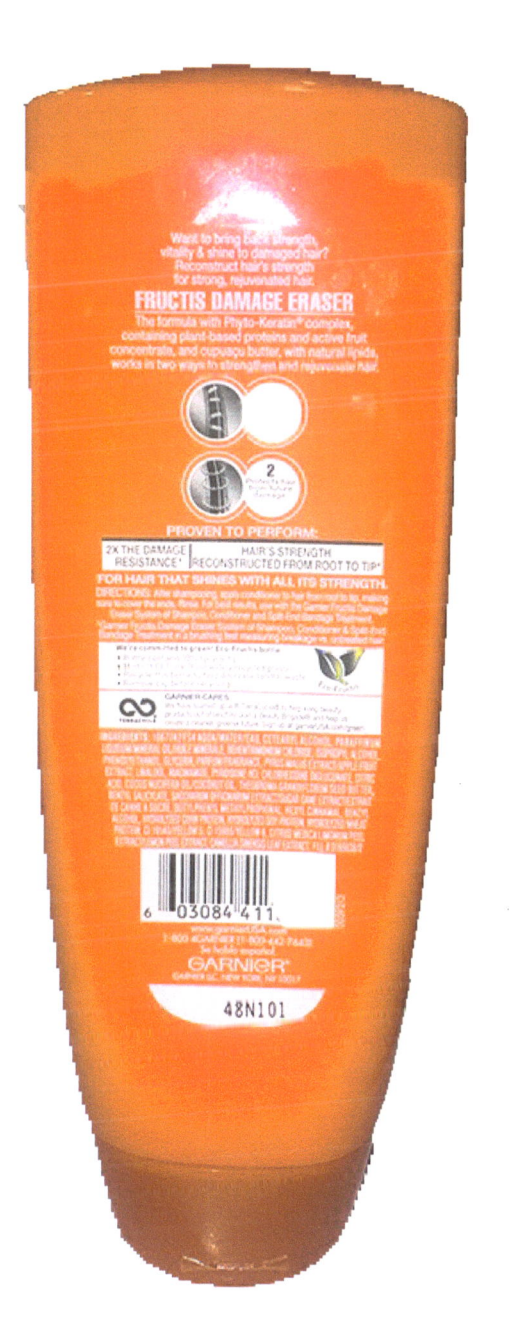

Want to bring back strength,
vitality & shine to damaged hair?
Reconstruct hair's strength
for strong, rejuvenated hair.

**FRUCTIS DAMAGE ERASER**

The formula with Phyto-Keratin® complex,
containing plant-based proteins and active fruit
concentrate, and cupuaçu butter, with natural lipids,
works in two ways to strengthen and rejuvenate hair.

**PROVEN TO PERFORM:**

| 2X THE DAMAGE RESISTANCE* | HAIR'S STRENGTH RECONSTRUCTED FROM ROOT TO TIP* |
|---|---|

**FOR HAIR THAT SHINES WITH ALL ITS STRENGTH.**

DIRECTIONS: After shampooing, apply conditioner to hair from root to tip, making
sure to cover the ends. Rinse. For best results, use with the Garnier Fructis Damage
Eraser System of Shampoo, Conditioner and Split-End Bandage Treatment.
*Garnier Fructis Damage Eraser System of Shampoo, Conditioner & Split-End
Bandage Treatment in a brushing test measuring breakage vs. untreated hair.

GARNIER CARES.

INGREDIENTS: ... AQUA/WATER/EAU, CETEARYL ALCOHOL, PARAFFINUM
LIQUIDUM/MINERAL OIL/HUILE MINÉRALE, BEHENTRIMONIUM CHLORIDE, ISOPROPYL ALCOHOL,
PHENOXYETHANOL, GLYCERIN, PARFUM/FRAGRANCE, PRUNUS AMYGDALUS... APPLE FRUIT
EXTRACT, LINALOOL, NIACINAMIDE, PYRIDOXINE HCl, CHLORHEXIDINE DIGLUCONATE, CITRIC
ACID, COCOS NUCIFERA OIL/COCONUT OIL, THEOBROMA GRANDIFLORUM SEED BUTTER,
BENZYL SALICYLATE, SACCHARUM OFFICINARUM EXTRACT/SUGAR CANE EXTRACT/EXTRAIT
DE CANNE À SUCRE, BUTYLPHENYL METHYLPROPIONAL, HEXYL CINNAMAL, BENZYL
ALCOHOL, HYDROLYZED CORN PROTEIN, HYDROLYZED SOY PROTEIN, HYDROLYZED WHEAT
PROTEIN, CI 19140/YELLOW 5, CI 15985/YELLOW 6, CITRUS MEDICA LIMONUM PEEL
EXTRACT/LEMON PEEL EXTRACT, CAMELLIA SINENSIS LEAF EXTRACT. F.I.L. B #####/#.

www.garnierUSA.com
1-800-4GARNIER (1-800-442-7643)
Se habla español.

**GARNIER®**
GARNIER LLC, NEW YORK, NY 10017

6 03084 411

48N101

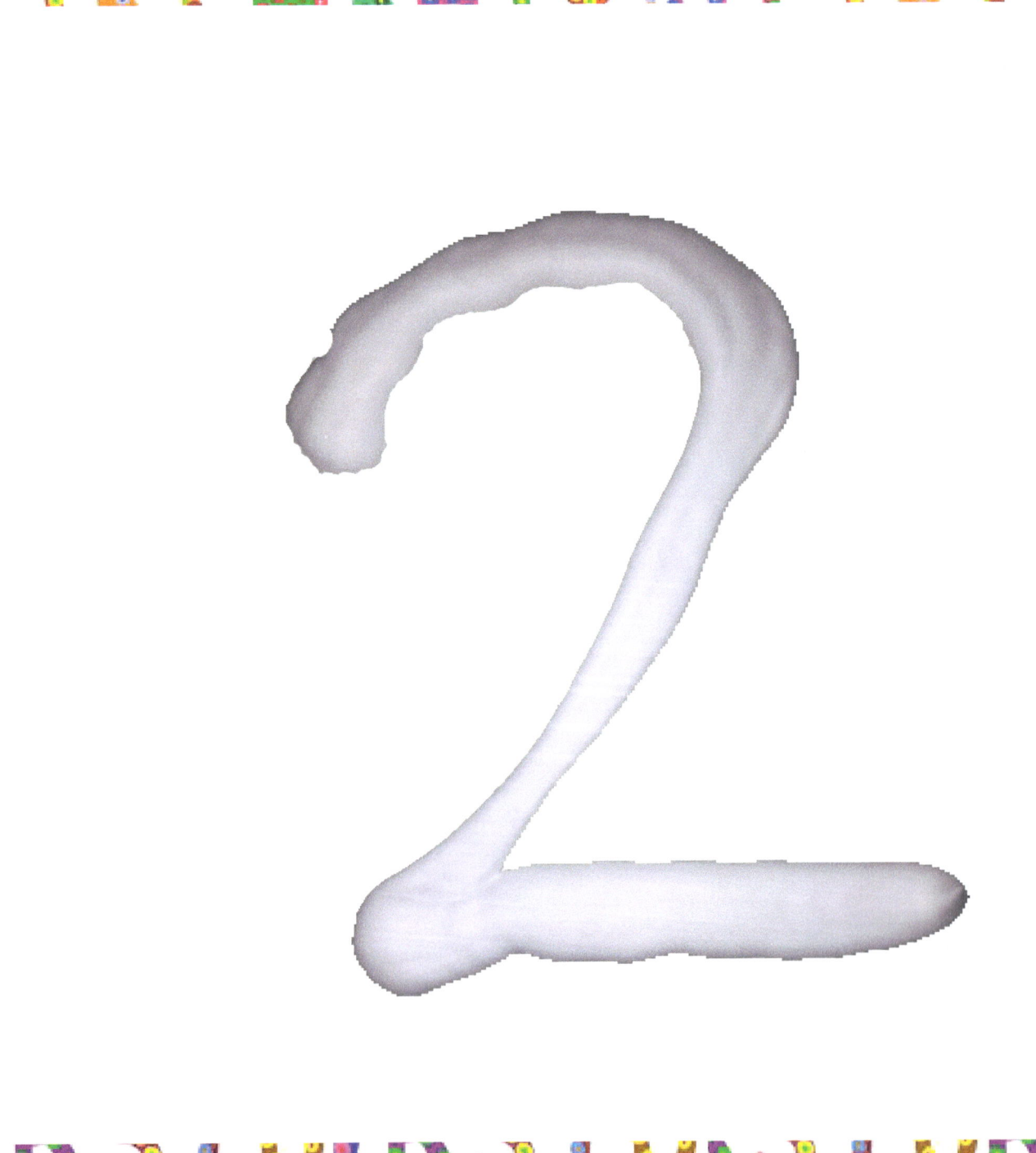

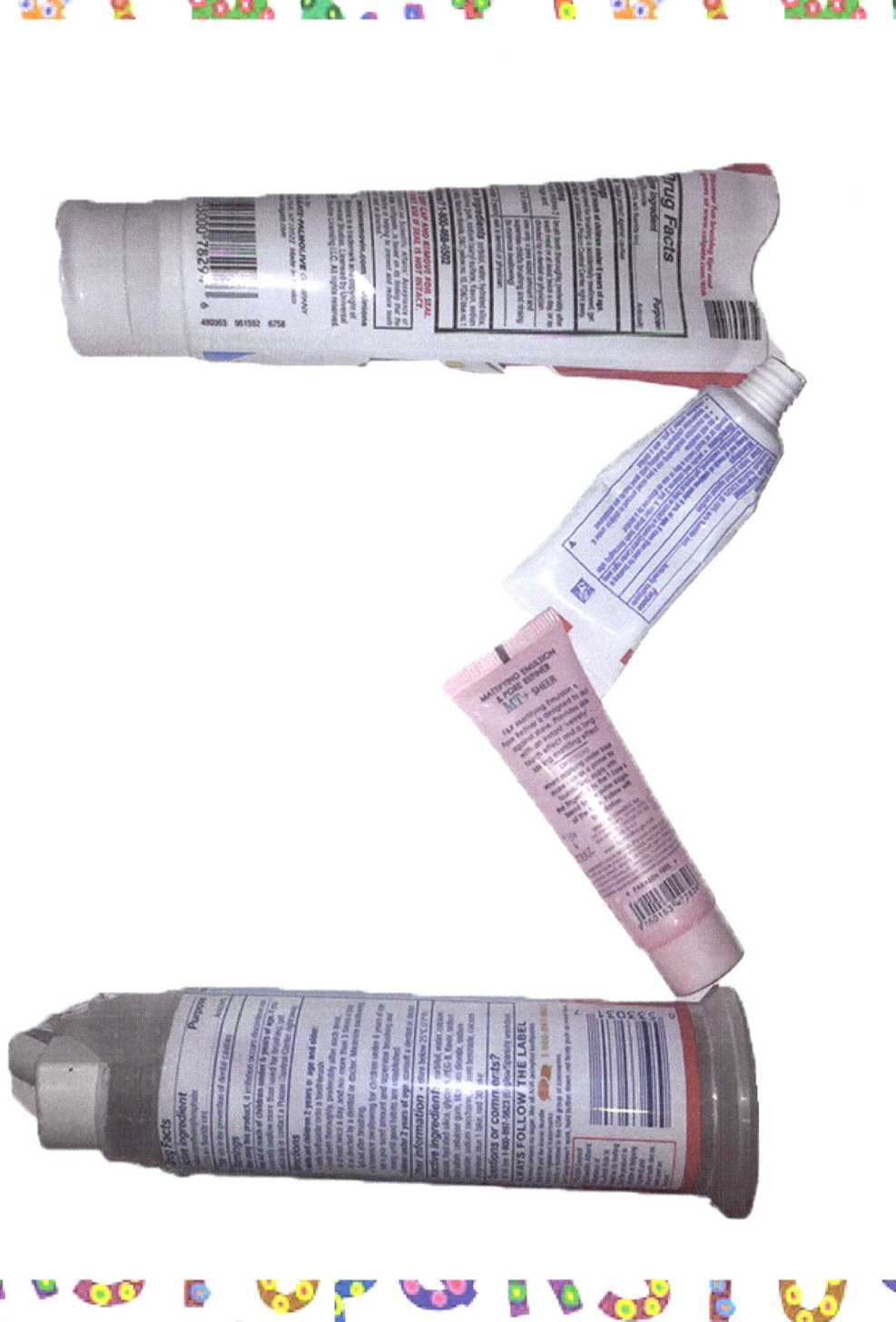

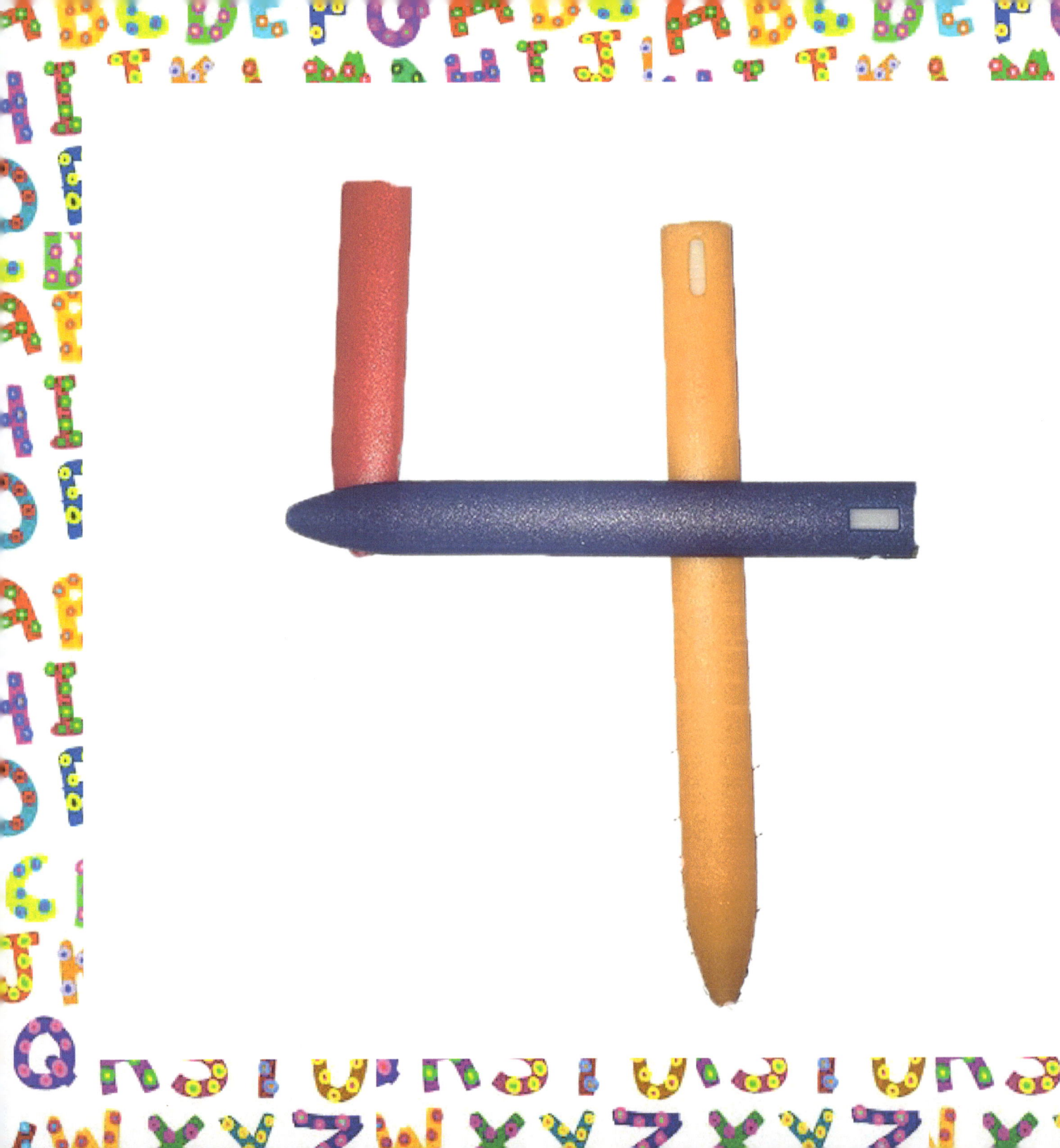

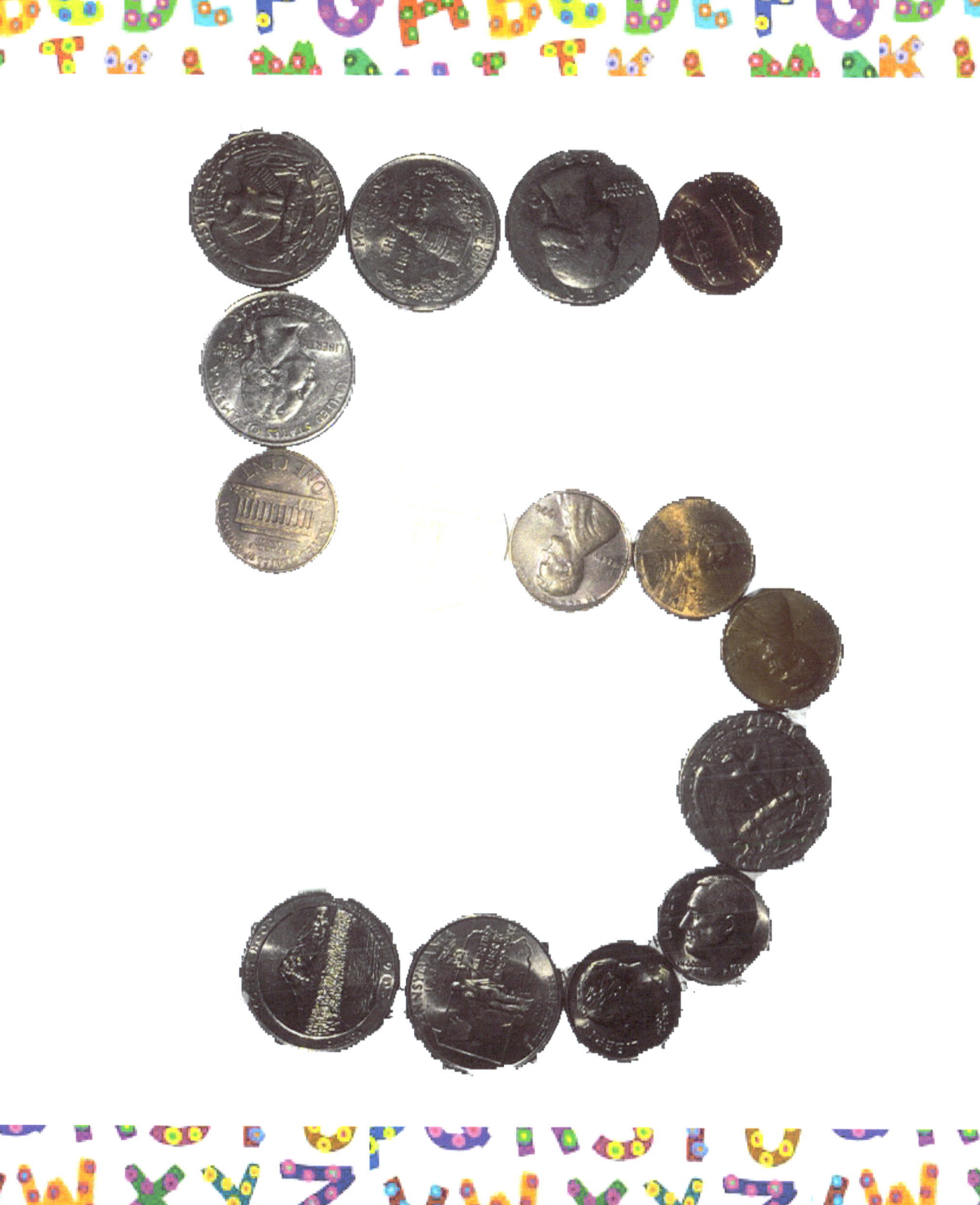

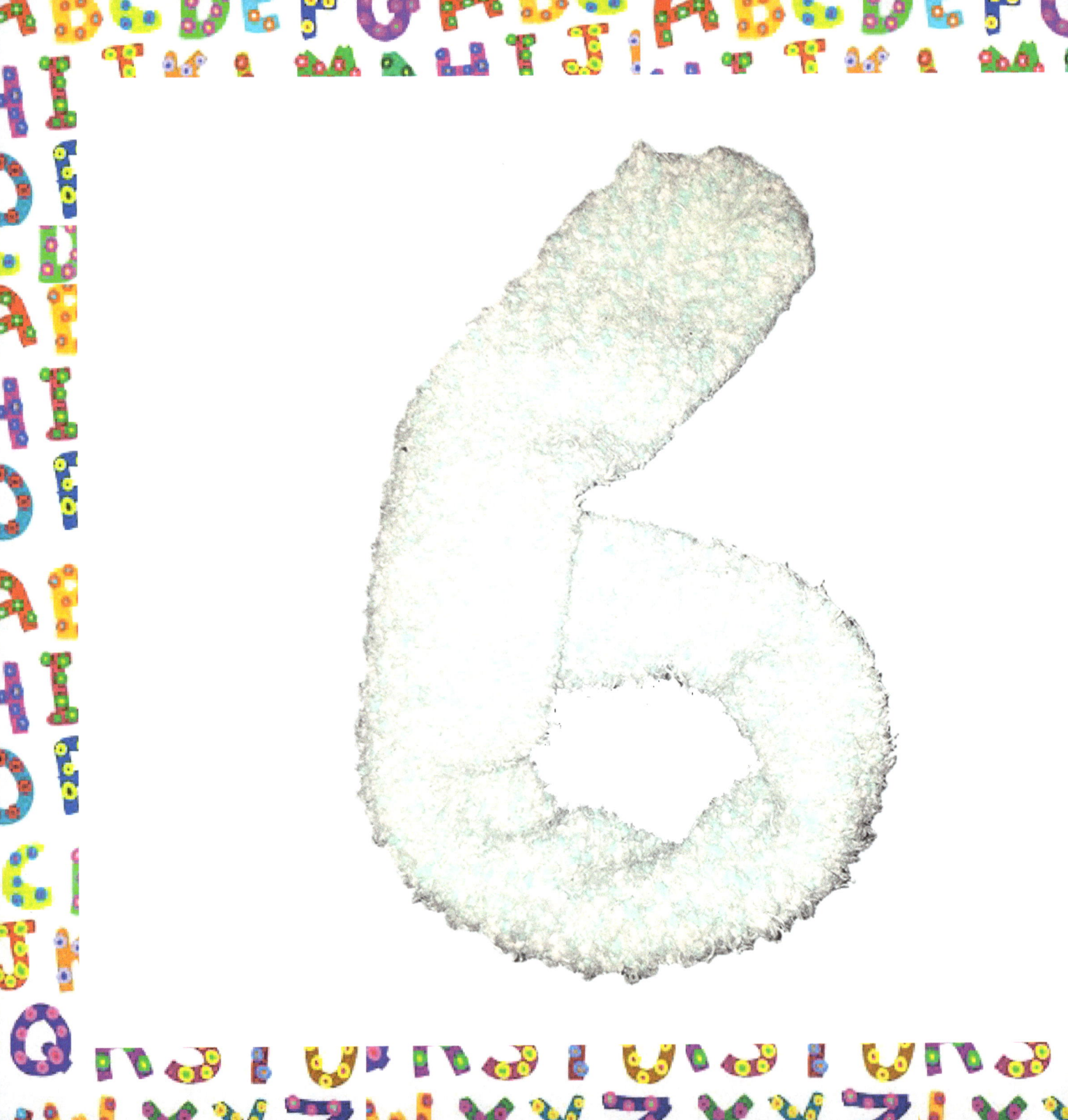

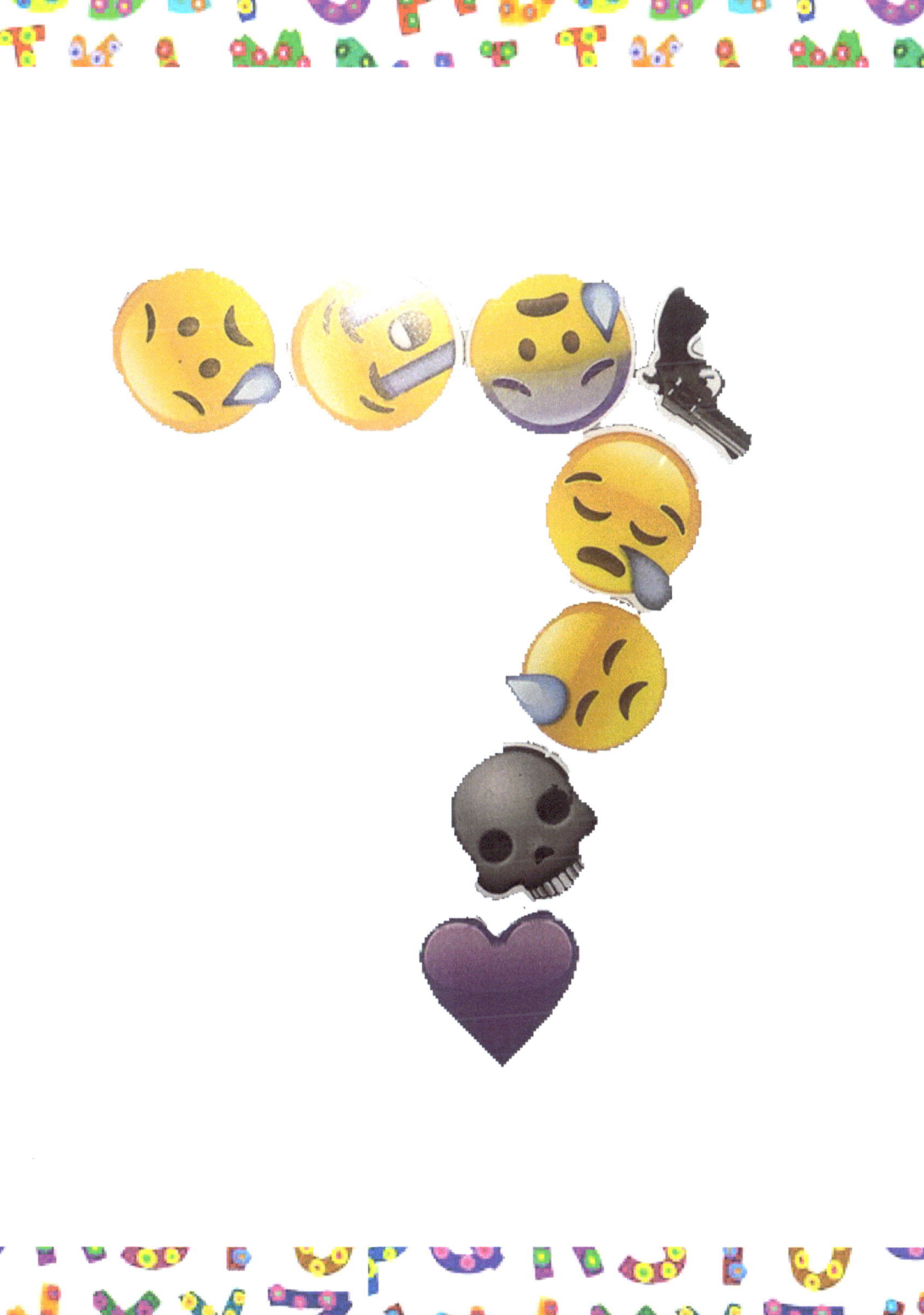

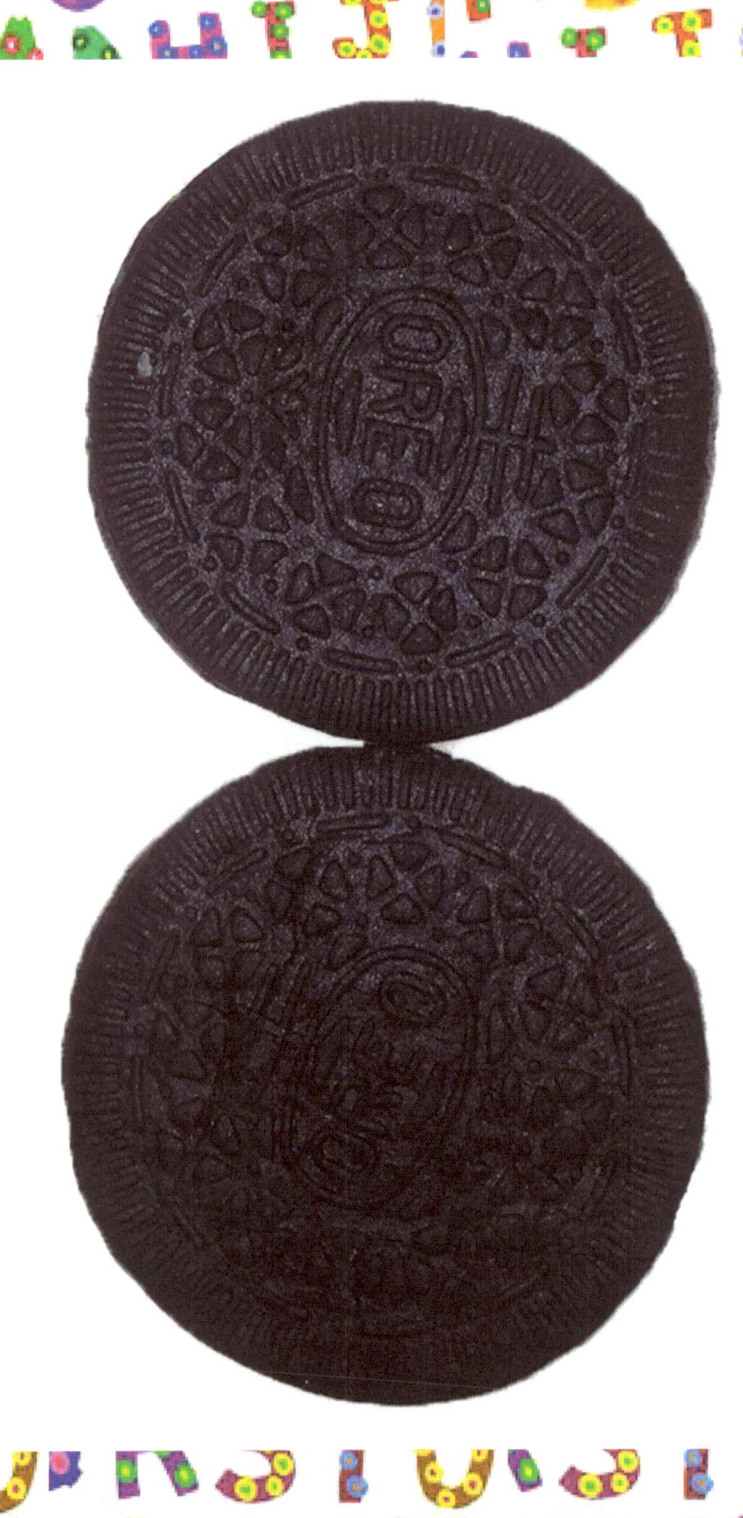

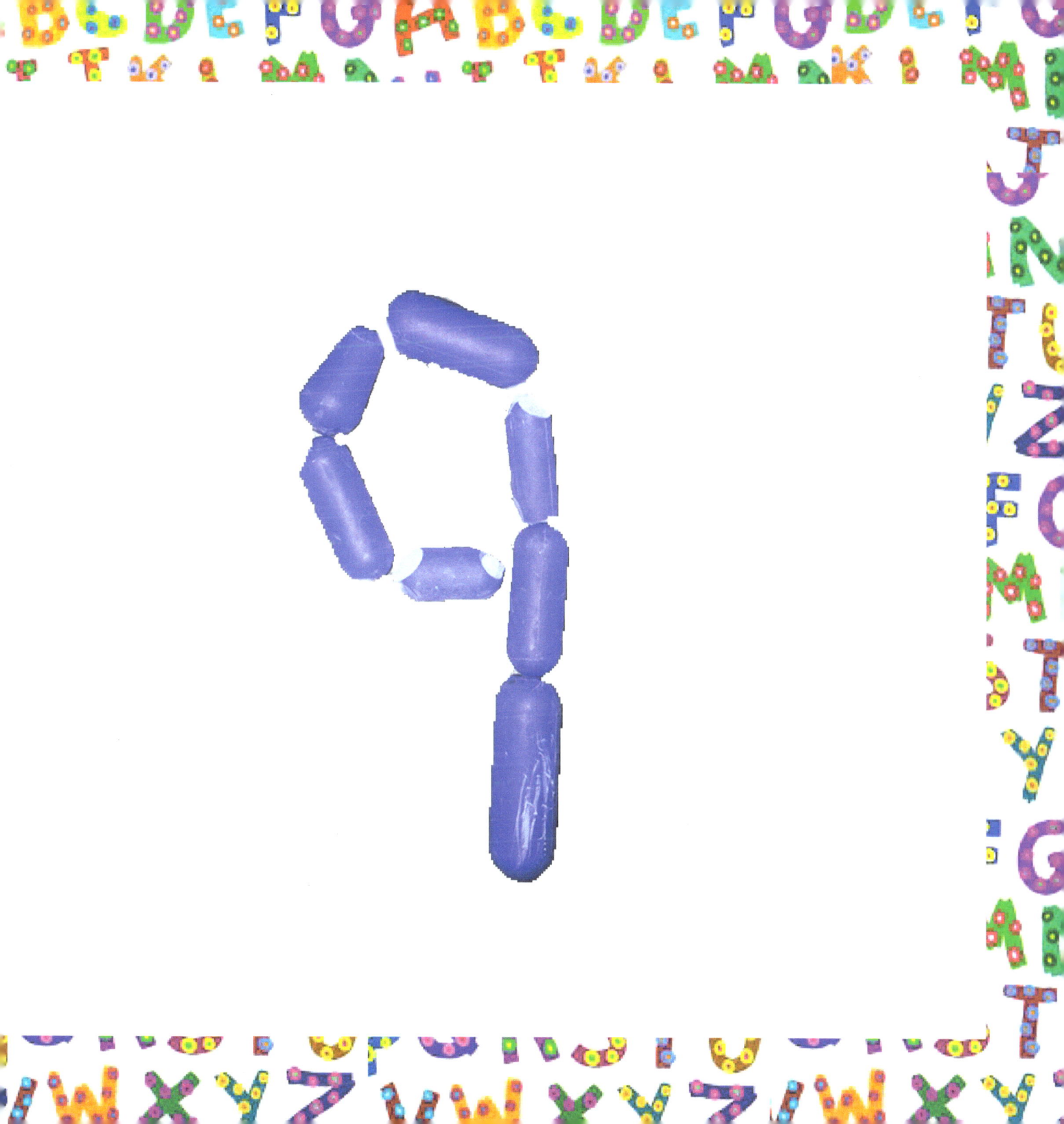

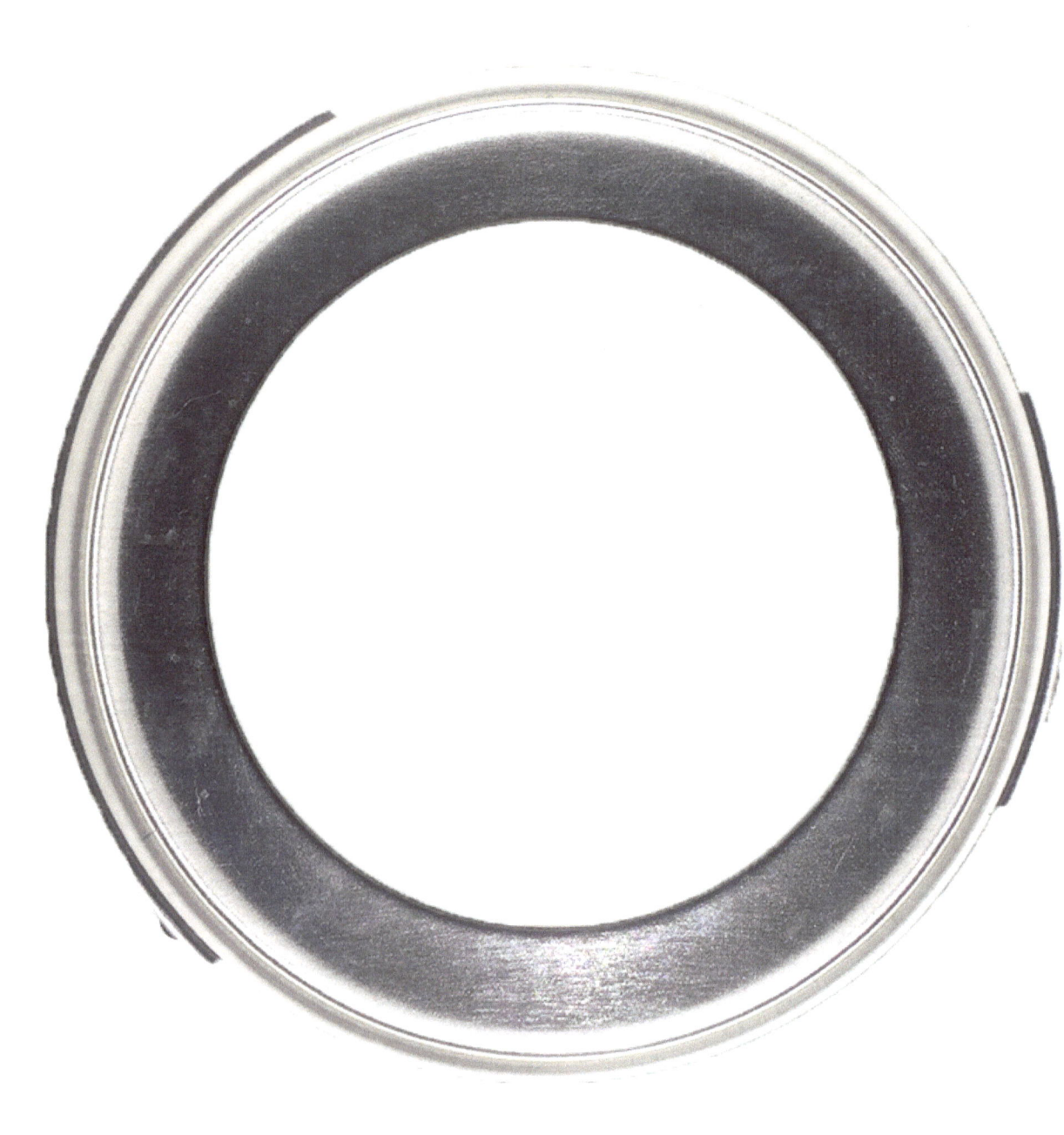

www.ingramcontent.com/pod-product-compliance
Lightning Source LLC
Chambersburg PA
CBHW050357180526
45159CB00005B/2056